1D

LIFE IN EDWARDIAN ENGLAND

Ascot, at the turn of the century

Life in
EDWARDIAN
ENGLAND

ROBERT CECIL

English Life Series
EDITED BY PETER QUENNELL

LONDON: B. T. Batsford Ltd
NEW YORK: G. P. Putnam's Sons

First published 1969

© Robert Cecil, 1969

7134 1460 x

Made and printed in Great Britain
by Jarrold & Sons Ltd, Norwich
for the publishers
B. T. BATSFORD LTD
4 Fitzhardinge Street, London W.1
G. P. PUTNAM'S SONS
200 Madison Avenue, New York, NY 10016

Preface

Writing social history of the present century is a fascinating, but sometimes perplexing, occupation; fascinating, because one gleans unsuspected information about the origins of familiar customs and institutions; perplexing, because one cannot be an expert on every aspect of life in an age of ever-growing specialisation. In preparing this volume, I have, therefore, been much indebted to other authors. Some of their names appear in the text or in the short bibliographical lists appended to each chapter; but many have been omitted in the interests of keeping these lists within reasonable bounds.

I am also grateful to many people who have kindly provided material or made helpful suggestions. Among them I should particularly like to mention here Mr L. E. Rowan Bentall and Mr G. B. L. Wilson (Ch. III); Mr Esmond Seal (Ch. IV); Mr E. J. T. Collins and Mrs T. H. Sutton (Ch. VI); Mr E. E. Y. Hales and Mr T. W. Slack (Ch. VII); and Mrs Stuart Stevenson and my wife (Ch. VIII).

Prices present a problem. They can mislead a reader; but it is sometimes necessary to quote them, in order to indicate relative values. The reader is recommended, if he wishes to arrive at modern equivalents, to multiply Edwardian prices on the scale proposed by Messrs Johnson, Whyman and Wykes in their *Short Economic and Social History of Twentieth Century Britain*. According to their calculation, if £1 purchased 20 shillings worth of goods in 1964, it would have purchased 110 shillings worth between 1900 and 1906. After the latter date a slow rise in prices set in up to the outbreak of the First World War.

ROBERT CECIL

University of Reading, Berkshire

Contents

Acknowledgment

The author and publisher wish to thank the following for permission to quote from the books listed below (page references are to *Life in Edwardian England*): M. K. Ashby, *Joseph Ashby of Tysoe*, Cambridge University Press, p. 156; Memorial Magazine to J. H. Badley, Bedales School, p. 149; W. N. P. Barbellion, *Journal of a Disappointed Man*, Chatto & Windus, p. 89; Lord Beveridge, *Power and Influence*, Hodder and Stoughton Ltd, pp. 26–7; Mark Bonham-Carter (ed.), *The Autobiography of Margot Asquith*, Eyre & Spottiswoode (Publishers) Ltd, and Houghton Mifflin Company, pp. 31–2, 33, 36; Sir Reader Bullard, *The Camels Must Go*, Faber & Faber Ltd, pp. 141, 151–2; Neville Cardus, *Autobiography*, Wm. Collins Sons & Co. Ltd, pp. 54, 191–2, 193–4, 198; Charles Chaplin, *My Autobiography*, The Bodley Head Ltd, pp. 63, 70, 133–4; R. S. Churchill, *Winston Churchill (Vol 1)*, Heinemann, p. 8; W. H. Davies, *Autobiography of a Super Tramp*, Mrs H. M. Davies and Jonathan Cape Ltd, p. 154; Lord Ernle, *English Farming Past and Present*, Heinemann, p. 118; Robert Graves, *Goodbye to all that*, Cassell & Co. Ltd, p.148; Kenneth Grahame, *Wind in the Willows*, p. 72; Graham Greene, *The Old School*, Jonathan Cape, p. 166; Peter Green, *Kenneth Grahame*, John Murray Ltd, and Harold Ober Associates, pp. 129, 132–3; L. E. Jones, *An Edwardian Youth*, Macmillan & Co. Ltd, St Martin's Press Inc, and The Macmillan Company of Canada pp. 103, 153, 161, 199; Sonia Keppel, *Edwardian Daughter*, copyright © 1958 by Sonia Keppel, Hamish Hamilton, London, pp. 45–6, 50, 158; Rudyard Kipling, *Centenary of Short Stories*, Mrs George Bambridge, pp. 88, 147; F. Lamb and H. Pickerton, *Locked-up Daughters*, Hodder & Stoughton, pp. 165–6; Margaret Lane, *Edgar Wallace*, Hamish Hamilton Ltd, p. 103; C. E. Lee, *Sixty Years of the Northern*, London Transport, pp. 84–5; Rosamond Lehmann, *The Red-Haired Miss Daintreys*, The Society of Authors and Miss Rosamond Lehmann, p. 138; Rosamond Lehmann, *The Swan in the Evening*, Wm. Collins & Sons, p. 133; Jack London, *People of the Abyss*, pp. 57–9, 93; *Letters of H. E. Luxmore*, Cambridge University Press, p. 146; Mackerness, *Journals of George Sturt*, Cambridge University Press, pp. 22, 29, 123, 124–5; Mrs C. F. G. Masterman, Article in *History Today*, November 1964, pp. 29–30, 35; Sir Philip Magnus, *Edward VII*, John Murray Ltd,

ACKNOWLEDGMENT

and E. P. Dutton & Co. Inc., pp. 13, 28, 34, 36; Colonel R. Mein-ertzhagen, *Diary of a Black Sheep*, Colonel Meinertzhagen's executors, p. 103; H. H. Munro, *Selected Short Stories of Saki*, p. 65; Harold Nicolson, *Small Talk*, Constable & Co. Ltd, p. 11; H. Owen, *Journey from Obscurity*, Oxford University Press, pp. 140–1; Sir Charles Petrie, *Scenes from Edwardian Life*, Eyre & Spottiswoode (Publishers) Ltd, and W. W. Norton & Company Inc., pp. 30–1, 40; Gwen Raverat, *Period Piece*, Faber & Faber Ltd, pp. 70, 157–8; B. Tillett, *Memories and Reflections*, Hutchinson Publishing Group Ltd, pp. 23–4, 40, 42; Flora Thompson, *Lark Rise to Candleford*, Oxford University Press, pp. 114, 125–6; H. G. Wells, *Tono-Bungay*, Executors of H. G. Wells and Wm. Collins & Sons, p. 12; H. G. Wells, *An Experiment in Autobiography*, permission of Professor G. P. Wells, Victor Gollancz Ltd, Collins-Knowlton-Wing Inc, and the Executors of the Estate of H. G. Wells. Copyright © 1934 by Herbert George (HG) Wells. Copyright renewed by George Philip Wells and Francis Richard Wells, pp. 25–26, 62, 71–2, 175; H. G. Wells, *The Soul of a Bishop*, p. 167; V. Sackville West, *The Edward-ians*, Mr Nigel Nicolson and Hogarth Press, pp. 120–1; F. White, *A Fire in the Kitchen*, J. M. Dent & Sons Ltd, p. 162; Sir L. Wood-ward, *Short Journey*, p. 144; K. Young, *A. J. Balfour*, G. Bell & Sons Ltd, p. 22.

The author and publishers would also like to thank the following for permission to reproduce the illustrations in this book: Bentalls for fig. 44; Bournemouth Public Libraries for fig. 77; British Transport Commission for fig. 62; J. Allan Cash for fig. 81; Curtis Brown Ltd. for fig. 47; William Gordon Davies for figs. 1, 6, 7, 10, 11, 20, 26, 33–5, 37, 38, 50, 59, 67–71, 73, 75, 112 and 113; English Folk and Dance Society for fig. 85; E. & R. Garrould Ltd. for fig. 103; Anthony Glyn for fig. 111; Hodder and Stoughton Limited for fig. 94; Hulton Press for fig. 120; Lanchester Motor Co. Ltd for fig. 49; London Express News and Feature Services for fig. 115; London School of Economics (Passfield Trust) for fig. 16; Mansell Collection for figs. 2, 5, 14, 15, 17–19, 21, 23–5, 28, 29, 43, 55, 56, 60, 61, 72, 74, 76, 88–90, 96, 100–2, 104, 106–8, 118, 119, 121–3 and 129; George A. Oliver for fig. 48; Radio Times Hulton Picture Library for figs. 4, 8, 9, 12, 22, 27, 30–2, 36, 40, 46, 51–4, 58, 63, 65, 66, 78–80, 82, 87, 91, 92, 95, 99, 105, 109, 110, 114, 116, 117, 124, 125, 127 and 128; Ramsey & Musprat for fig. 84, Science Museum for figs. 64 and 83; Tate Gallery for fig. 86; Frederick Warne Ltd for fig. 93.

The Illustrations

ix

THE ILLUSTRATIONS

The King in Orbit

Historians, obliged as they are to divide history into arbitrary sections, may sometimes be tempted to plead in justification arguments more impressive than those of expediency and convenience. This temptation certainly affects the historian of the Edwardian period, for which it is possible to claim an unusual degree of coherence. First and most obviously, the reign of King Edward VII spanned the first decade of a new century after the longest reign in English history had ended. If we add on four more years, in which certain characteristic features of Edward's reign further developed and displayed themselves, we come to a natural watershed in the First World War. Edward's reign was, in this sense, an interlude between two wars, each of which in different ways had a fundamental influence on the life of this country. The statement that England after the 1914–18 war was never the same again requires no proof; it is illustrated by the popular belief that the Edwardian era was a Golden Age. The validity of this belief will be examined in the pages which follow; but it must be said at the outset that the Boer War, which ushered in Edward's reign, marked it with a leaden rather than a golden touch.

The end of the Boer War was already a foregone conclusion when Edward came to the throne in January 1901; but it dragged on until the final surrender on 31 May 1902, causing Britain ever-increasing embarrassment and emphasizing her isolation and unpopularity in the world. It became, therefore, an imperative of foreign policy, to which the King himself made a unique contribution, to make some friends and, in

A batch of recruits for the army, 1900

particular, to acquire allies against the potential hostility of
Germany. Moreover, the long war against a numerically
inferior foe had brought to light grave defects in the
organization and equipment of the Army and the direction of
strategy and training by the War Office; apart from a few
senior officers, who felt themselves exposed to criticism and
cherished a system that had permitted them to achieve seniority
with such small exertion, the demand for reform was universal.
In this field also the King played a highly effective part. The
rejection on health grounds of large numbers of recruits
stimulated public awareness that all was not well in the slums
and rural hovels of Merrie England. Here, too, Edward was
abreast of the best opinion of his time; he was conscious of his

2

duties as a slum landlord and took a notable interest throughout his life in medical research and the foundation of hospitals.

If Britain's imperial greatness seemed threatened by military failure and the rise to Great Power status of Germany, the United States and Japan, it was also being undermined from within. Although at one end of the spectrum of opinion the Boer War had given rise to outbursts of Jingoism, culminating in the popular hysteria occasioned by the relief of Ladysmith and Mafeking, at the other extremity more thoughtful elements had begun to have serious doubts about Britain's mission in Africa and Asia. Indeed, the Liberal Party was split; the Imperialist wing was led by Rosebery, Asquith, Grey and Haldane; the Little-Englanders included not only the young

3

British troops storming the kopje

Lloyd George, but also Sir William Harcourt and John Morley.

The collective personality of British Imperialism embodied many different elements: the sincere missionary, the less scrupulous trader, the young administrator with a sense of service and the 'jelly-bellied flag-wagger', who wanted to see more red on the map, all played a role. In the late Victorian era religious zeal had waned and, with it, much of the missionary motive; but there remained in many circles a firm belief in Britain's civilizing mission. When an enterprising young lieutenant in the 4th Queen's Own Hussars, named Winston L. Spencer Churchill, wrote a book about an action on the North-West frontier of India, entitled *The Story of the Malakand Field Force*, he prefaced it with the following description of frontier wars from the lips of the Prime Minister, Lord Salisbury: 'They are but the surf that marks the edge and the advance of the wave of civilisation.' The sentiment was typical of the period before the Boer War; but that war and the 'methods of barbarism' (as Campbell-Bannerman called them), which had been necessary to bring it to an end, had opened many people's eyes to the high price of civilization in terms of human suffering. If the end was, indeed, civilization, was it right to advance the cause by barbarous means?

These were not the only misgivings. The religious doubts that had long since begun to vex the Victorians were growing more acute. The strength of the Church of England had always been in country districts; but over three-quarters of the population now lived in towns. How were churches and a trained clergy to be provided to meet the insistent needs of the industrial cities? The House of Lords, that bastion of the Established Church, could veto the Liberal Education Bill, providing for non-denominational religious teaching in State schools; but it could not relight the candles that burned ever more dimly on the altars. Doubt had infected even the Non-conformist middle classes. Was it certain that the theory of the self-perpetuating evolution of the human species (mistakenly ascribed to Darwin) also applied in the sphere of morals? Was there perhaps a flaw in the traditional Calvinist assumption that a man who was saved would prosper? If prosperity was rooted in virtue, how was it that in Britain, as the few became richer, the worse became the conditions in which the impoverished majority lived?

'*Came the Whisper, came the Vision.*' From *Kipling's* Song of the English

5

Slums, slag-heaps, malnutrition and tuberculosis did not look like the rewards of national virtue; they were more suggestive of the wages of sin.

The voice of social conscience, never silent in the Victorian era, became very much louder in Edward's reign; it also became politically effective. Although death duties had first been imposed in 1894 and income tax had become an inescapable feature of Budgets, the ruling classes had never consciously or explicitly accepted the principle of transferring wealth from one section of the population to another by means of fiscal legislation. Moreover, land was still sacrosanct and brought political power with it. Robert Blake writes in his *Disraeli*: 'As late as 1870 four hundred peers were reckoned to own over one-sixth of the whole surface of the country.' The House of Lords was the expression of their political power and, when it rejected Lloyd George's 'People's Budget', it was the entire social order that was at stake; not only fiscal policy was called in question, but also the hereditary principle. The election slogan, 'Peers Against People', as used at the hustings by Lloyd George and Winston Churchill, did not prove as immediately efficacious as they had hoped; but the great issue, once raised, could not be put to sleep.

Uncertainty and indignation fermented in men's minds in these years; in comparison the mid-Victorian era had been one of assurance and relative tranquillity. Problems, to be sure, abounded; but eminent Victorians were confident that, even if solutions had not yet been found, solutions existed. Man was a rational animal and, on the whole, a moral one; he would find a way; even lasting peace between nations was not impossible. Stability had been the keynote of Victoria's long reign; even if its end had not happened to coincide with the birth of a new century, men would have felt change in the air and the stirring of new ideas. In some quarters there was almost a sigh of relief at her death; but the stronger feeling was that expressed, in almost identical words, by Henry James and Marie Corelli: 'We all feel motherless today'.

The Queen died at Osborne in the Isle of Wight and after she had lain in state there for ten days her mortal remains were

Edward and the Kaiser following the gun carriage at Queen Victoria's funeral

borne to Portsmouth in the royal yacht *Alberta* between two
great lines of warships extending for five miles. As the sun went
down and the minute guns boomed out, the naval cortège
passed on its way and was swallowed up in the mist of the early
dusk of February. The old Queen was dead and the Victorian
era had died with her. Many of her subjects saw more of the
pomp of monarchy at her death than they had seen in her lifetime. Apart from her drive to St Paul's through cheering
crowds on the occasion of her Diamond Jubilee, the Queen
had been very much of a recluse. She had spent much of her
time at the extremities of her realm—at Balmoral and at
Osborne; otherwise she had scarcely travelled. Court life had
been formal, exclusive and insufferably wearisome. Edward, in
common with most of the Queen's subjects, believed that his
mother's insistence on her privacy was ill-advised. He was himself gregarious and mobile by nature and he saw no reason to
change his habits when he became King. It was not enough to
be a King; he must be seen to be King. The fact that he looked
like a King was an additional argument.

7

Edward's Coronation provided the first opportunity for a display of royalty on parade; the date, 26 June 1902, was fixed, and elaborate preparations were made. Crown Princes and Heirs Apparent steamed into Victoria Station and later sat down to an immense banquet. It proved to be the only ceremony in which they took part. Edward was suffering from appendicitis and, after putting off his doctors as long as he dared in order to avoid disappointing his subjects, he finally submitted to an emergency operation. The mountain of food cooked for the Imperial and Royal guests had to be disposed of and the King's chef later recorded: 'It was the poor of Whitechapel and not the foreign kings, princes and diplomats who had the Consommé de faisan aux quenelles, Côtelettes de bécassines à la Souvaroff and many other dishes. . . .' But 2,500 quails were put on ice for future use. The Coronation, which eventually took place on 9 August, was mainly a domestic event. The common people cheered the procession and got drunk in the pubs and sang 'Dolly Gray' and 'The Honeysuckle and the Bee'. Wealthy people gave succulent supper-parties; Rosa Lewis cooked 21 of them in that one week. Inside Westminster Abbey a box was specially constructed to accommodate friends of the King, such as Sarah Bernhardt and Mrs George Keppel, whom protocol would otherwise have kept at a distance; it was called by some flippant observers 'the King's Loose Box'. Nobody entertained any doubts that not only a new reign, but also a new social era had begun. Young Winston Churchill was one of those who wondered what would happen next.

I am curious to know about the King. . . . Will he sell his horses and scatter his Jews or will Reuben Sassoon be enshrined among the crown jewels and other regalia? Will he become desperately serious? Will he continue to be friendly to you? Will the Keppel be appointed First Lady of the Bedchamber?

The 'Marlborough House set' had been composed in the first instance of members of society congenial to the Prince of

Wales who found, as he did, that the atmosphere at Court was tedious and restrictive. Edward had soon begun to introduce into his circle not only American heiresses, opera singers and professional beauties, like Lily Langtry, but also wealthy men from commerce and the City, who had never before made the transition in one generation to the highest level of society. There were, of course, a few exclusive hostesses who held out against the invasion; but if they had thought that Edward, on ascending the throne, would

Lily Langtry

abandon his friends, they were soon mistaken. Their scorn for the newcomers was shared by the German Emperor who, hearing that his uncle was at Cowes with Sir Thomas Lipton, referred to him as 'boating with his grocer'. Edward continued to consort unperturbed not only with Lord Iveagh, the brewer, and Sir Blundell Maple, the furniture manufacturer, but also with Jewish financiers, such as Baron Hirsch, Sir Ernest Cassel and Sir Alfred Beit, whose presence at Court offended the anti-Semitism of the day. Edward valued their financial advice and encouraged their philanthropy; his patronage was a strong and necessary solvent of prejudice.

Edward liked being King and rightly held himself well qualified for the functions he had to perform; but he did not intend to allow his duties to exclude his pleasures. His subjects could not *en masse* join him shooting at Sandringham, yachting in the Mediterranean, playing bridge at the country houses of his friends, or setting himself up for another year of high living by taking the cure at Marienbad; but there was one pleasure that he could share with his people: horse-racing. Every year he attended the meetings at Ascot, Epsom and Goodwood and the colours of his stable—purple, scarlet and gold—were known to all. His victory with Minoru in the Derby of 1909 was the high point of his popularity and Epsom Downs resounded with the loyal cry, 'Good old Teddy!'. On 6 May 1910, when he was manifestly dying, the news was brought to him that his horse Witch of the Air had won the 4.15 at Kempton Park.

In his last year as Prince of Wales, Edward had attended 86 public functions, exclusive of his appearances at race-meetings, the opera and similar social events. He continued to make these appearances; indeed, at least one journalist assigned to covering the royal presence at functions in the London area thought his sense of duty excessive. 'I think the King goes about a d—— sight too much,' observed Edgar Wallace, who at that time was working for the *Daily Mail*, 'and I wish to heaven he would give up processing; one gets very tired to fossicking around after the old cove.' In July a few days would be spent by the King in an important industrial area. There were at all times, of course, regular visits to the country houses of his loyal subjects, where amateur theatricals were an obligatory part of the programme. The monarchy had become peripatetic to a degree scarcely known since the Middle Ages.

Edward winning the Derby with his horse, Minoru

Edward with friends at Goodwood House in 1906. Mrs Keppel is seated on the extreme left

To entertain the King was a formidable undertaking. The guest list required careful preparation and, if Queen Alexandra was not to be of the party, the allocation of bedrooms and dressing-rooms needed special advice and discretion. The royal progress to Chatsworth, Crewe Hall or West Dean Park included a retinue of at least 12 equerries and servants, or if the Queen accompanied the King, 18 persons. It was a strain even at Chatsworth, where as many as 470 people had been accommodated at one time. The Edwardian week-end, which formed the major part of the royal progress, has been described by none more vividly than Sir Harold Nicolson and his wife, Victoria Sackville-West.

Tea was served in the blue gallery. There were little ginger biscuits which one could only get from Biarritz and of which one kept a store in case the King came. All Edwardian houses kept stores of things like ginger biscuits and aubergines and French pâtisseries and bath salts in case the King came. And come he did. He came over and over again. And on Monday morning other people would read all about it in the *Morning Post*.

Most of the great country houses had ceased to fulfil any economic or social purpose and, although they still seemed to dominate the rural communities, of which they had once been the central feature, their organic relationship to the countryside was fast disappearing under the influence of other changes,

11

especially the revolution in transport and human mobility. Some of the old houses had already passed into the hands of City magnates and others, to whom H. G. Wells applied the term 'pseudomorphs'; that is, those who no longer performed the function of the former owners, whose way of life they aped from Friday to Monday.

The great houses stand in their parks still, the cottages cluster respectfully on their borders, touching their eaves with their creepers, the English countryside . . . persists obstinately in looking what it was. It is like an early day in a fine October. The hand of change rests on it all, unfelt, unseen; resting for a while, as it were half-reluctantly, before it grips and ends the thing for ever.

If it seems to us today that Edward spent an undue proportion of his time in the company of this small, exclusive section of his people, we must remember that they were not only his friends and the upper crust of society; they were also the ruling class in a sense in which this category has never existed since. (The modern 'Establishment' is a different concept.) Members of these families were still powerful in public life, particularly in diplomacy and the armed services. These latter fields of activity were those in which the King was chiefly interested and, as a good constitutional monarch, he exerted his very considerable influence through those of his subjects who held responsible positions.

In the first decade of this century personal diplomacy was pursued in a more leisurely, discreet and effective way than is possible at the brief, widely advertised 'summit conferences' that take place today. Edward was particularly well placed to bring his strong personality to bear upon the diplomatic problems of his time. He was the 'Uncle of Europe'. The German Kaiser was his nephew; the Queens of Spain and Norway were his nieces; Queen Alexandra's nephews were on the thrones of Denmark and Greece; the Tsar of Russia was also her nephew and his Tsarina was Edward's niece. In these days, when dynasties have either disappeared or ceased to wield

A house party at Windsor, 1907. From left to right: Queen Ena of Spain, Edward, the Empress of Germany, the Kaiser, Queen Alexandra, the Queen of Portugal, King Alfonso of Spain, Queen Maud of Norway

power, it requires an effort of imagination to understand how important these relationships could be in maintaining the 'concert of Europe'. It is true that the most important of these family connections, that with the Kaiser, was a diplomatic failure; but Edward, resigning himself to the impossibility of calming his nephew Wilhelm's aggressive tendencies, exploited with much more success his personal contacts with the timid and indecisive Tsar, whose adherence to the *entente* with France was essential to Britain's security.

Because Edward, unlike his fellow monarchs, reigned, but did not rule, he did not initiate foreign policy; in the first year of his reign he was a passive spectator of the tentative efforts of Lord Lansdowne and Joseph Chamberlain to reach an understanding with Germany. It was in exploring the alternative of an alliance with France that the King played his most significant role. In April 1900 at the height of the Boer War, when the Fashoda incident was still fresh in French minds, hostility to Britain was so rampant that Edward, who was still Prince of Wales, was obliged to abandon his intention to attend the opening of the International Exhibition in Paris. In 1903,

13

Edward acknowledging the crowd at Longchamps

however, he insisted on visiting Paris against the cautious advice of the Foreign Office and within a few days had succeeded in converting the attitude of sullen or indifferent Frenchmen to one of open enthusiasm for the British monarchy, if not for the British people. It was a foundation on which his Ministers could built in their attempt to fortify their country against the dangerous isolation in which Lord Salisbury had left her.

After diplomacy it was the Army and Navy which chiefly benefited from the King's interest. His first Secretary of State for War was St John Brodrick, who felt at the time of his transfer to the India Office in 1903 that his position had been undermined by Lord Esher, the King's influential private adviser on military matters. Nevertheless Brodrick, who had no reason to revere the King's memory, later paid tribute to 'the impetus which King Edward gave to all military progress' and singled out the 'reform of the medical system, which he pressed forward from the first day of his reign'. Edward, who in letters to Esher referred to the War Office as 'a mutual admiration society' and an 'Augean Stable', pressed his proposals for reform so vigorously that Balfour appointed a War Office Reconstitution Committee, usually known as the Esher Committee. Its report, published in 1904, led to the creation of the Army Council and the General Staff, as well as the division of Great Britain into seven territorial commands. Although the abolition at the same time of the post of Commander-in-Chief offended the incumbent, Lord Roberts, and the aspirant, Lord Kitchener, these reforms were generally recognized as long overdue.

When in 1905 Campbell-Bannerman came to power, his reforming Secretary of State for War, Haldane, had the backing of the King in his reorganization of the Regular Army.

Edward was less enthusiastic about the subsequent plan to merge the Militia, Yeomanry and Volunteers in one Territorial Army, but he continued to stand by Haldane against the economizing zeal of Lloyd George and Winston Churchill. Haldane's project, which had considerable social implications, was opposed by Roberts, who formed the National Service League to advocate conscription. Voluntary duty had a long and honourable history. The Train bands of London in Cromwell's time, the Armed Associations of the eighteenth century and the Volunteer Movement of the Napoleonic Wars had all been constituted for home defence; but neither the training nor the equipment of the nineteenth-century mounted Yeomanry and Volunteer infantry was adequate to enable the Regular Army to rely on their support in time of war. Haldane combined them in the Territorial Army, which came into existence in 1908. He reinforced the territorial links of this new force and his hand was strengthened by the action of the King in summoning his Lords-Lieutenant of Counties to Buckingham Palace and enjoining co-operation upon them. The landed interest, however, was too deeply entrenched in the Militia, which rejoiced in an exclusive officer caste. It resisted integration and had to be reconstituted in the form of a Special Reserve.

If Edward's interest in naval reform is even better known, this is mainly because of his friendship with its colourful protagonist, Admiral Sir John Fisher, who was determined that the Navy should not suffer as the Army had done by having to learn painful lessons in the hard school of war. His struggle to modernize the Navy in peacetime and force it to apply recent scientific innovations was resisted by a group of senior officers led by Admiral Lord Charles Beresford. This tug-of-war gained added piquancy from the fact that Beresford had formerly been a confidant of Edward, when he was Prince of Wales, but had for some years been alienated from him as a result of a *cause célèbre* in which the leading lady, sought after by both men, had been the beautiful Lady Brooke, later Countess of Warwick. Although Beresford was baulked of his hope of succeeding Fisher as First Sea Lord, the backing of the Conservative

Opposition enabled him to force Asquith to appoint a sub-committee of the Committee of Imperial Defence to inquire into allegations of naval unpreparedness. A pressure group, calling itself the Imperial Maritime League, demanded Fisher's resignation, which followed in 1910. Fisher never ceased to assert that the King had been his greatest supporter and 'the Dukes and Duchesses' his chief opponents. Winston Churchill later summed up his achievements: 'There is no doubt whatever that Fisher was right in nine-tenths of what he fought for.'

In these military and naval controversies Edward displayed his capacity to keep abreast of the more advanced thought of his generation. In other areas he showed himself more in harmony with the conservative elements. He was, for example, antipathetic to women's suffrage. He was a firm supporter of the hereditary principle in public life, though receptive to the idea of life peerages. When the House of Lords began to reject or drastically amend Liberal legislation, he took the view that his Ministers were fully entitled to criticize the Upper House, but should not advocate its abolition. He attempted to bring about a compromise over the Lords' emasculation of Augustine Birrell's Education Bill and deplored their refusal to pass the Licensing Bill of 1908. When the final clash came over the 'People's Budget', he tried to persuade Balfour and Lansdowne to modify their opposition. He died before the final decision had to be taken on Asquith's proposal to overcome obstruction by a massive creation of Liberal peers.

Admiral Fisher

Though he favoured hereditary authority, Edward's attitude towards its foes was not as dogmatic and inflexible as his mother's had been. He admired the ability of Sir Charles Dilke, who had offended Queen Victoria by expressing republican sentiments, and he continued

16

Lady Warwick and her son

his friendship with Lady Warwick after her open espousal of socialism. He defended Fisher against his aristocratic enemies, although on one occasion he chided him for being a socialist, after Fisher had proposed that naval cadets at Osborne and Dartmouth should be educated at the expense of the State. As Prince of Wales he had been glad to sit on the Royal Commission on the Aged Poor with two Members of Parliament recently recruited from the working class, Henry Broadhurst and Joseph Arch; he lived to see old people's hardships alleviated by Lloyd George's Old Age Pensions Act. Though not an imaginative man, Edward had more sympathy for the suffering of the poor than many of his wealthy subjects, who, like him, had more often been victims of repletion than of hunger.

The humanitarian aspect of Edward's character is best illustrated by his zeal for improved medical services not only in the Army but in the country as a whole. As Prince of Wales, he had set aside funds collected on the occasion of his mother's Diamond Jubilee in order to expand hospital services, for which the State at that time had no responsibility. King Edward's Hospital Fund, as it became known, trebled its income during his reign. A donation by Sir Ernest Cassel enabled the King to found a sanatorium for tuberculosis, which he opened at Midhurst in 1906. He claimed that his 'greatest ambition is not to quit this world till a real cure for cancer has been found'. He promoted this cause by persuading Cassel and Lord Iveagh to found a Radium Institute in London.

There were, of course, sides of Edward's character much less attractive than those depicted here. If we have not dwelt on them, it is not only because others have done so—perhaps even to excess—but also because they are not germane to our theme, which concerns his influence upon the life of his country and his claim to be regarded as representing the age that bears his name. The shortcomings of his private life were no worse than those of the ruling class of his day; they were writ large upon the minds of his contemporaries because of his eminence and the opportunities for self-indulgence that lay open to him. But his failings as a man detracted scarcely at all from his achievements as monarch. He was by nature impatient, but he executed the diplomatic tasks laid on him with tact and discretion. He was easily bored, but he never faltered in carrying out the tedious ceremonies of his high office. He was addicted to explosions of rage and crude practical jokes, but the circle of sufferers was no wider than his own entourage, which any member was free to leave at will. His public utterances were notably restrained, in comparison with those of his nephew, Kaiser Wilhelm. 'You cannot imagine what a Satan he is!' exclaimed the Kaiser, speaking of his uncle to astonished hearers. But when Edward died, the tribute paid to him by the Russian Foreign Minister was very different: 'We have lost the mainstay of our foreign policy.'

Edward's reputation has suffered from his neglect of art and literature, in which enduring traits of character are sometimes preserved. We tend to see him as he is recorded for us in the cartoons of Max Beerbohm, or as the 'corpulent voluptuary' of Rudyard Kipling's acid phrase. It is true that Edward was unmoved by the flowering of prose and painting which occurred in his reign and he did little or nothing to redeem its gross materialism; but Edward's indifference was common to the great majority of his subjects, rich and poor. In this

Edward at Biarritz

respect, too, he was a man of his time. 'The King is loved,' said Lord Granville, 'because he has all the faults of which the Englishman is accused.' This was a part of the secret of his power to extend his influence into all walks of life.

No courtier was better versed than the King in the punctilio of the Court; but beneath the trappings of the hereditary

The Kaiser, King George and Duke of Connaught, followed by the Duke of Cornwall (later the Duke of Windsor) and Prince Albert, walk behind Edward's coffin

sovereign there emerged—plain for all to see—the authentic human being, whose strength and weakness projected through the robes of state. In the final year of his life he made what was, perhaps, the last attempt of the monarch of these Islands to conduct himself in public as any ordinary person would do. Dozing on Worthing Pier, wrapped in a fur coat to keep out the winds of February, he awoke to find himself surrounded by so dense a crowd that the police had difficulty in forcing a way to his car through the cheering multitude. Returning on 27 April from his annual visit to Biarritz, he once more began to receive his Ministers in audience. On 29 April he attended a performance of *Siegfried* at Covent Garden and spent part of the next day, Sunday, touring his home farm at Sandringham. On 2 May he returned to Buckingham Palace and dined that evening, as he often did, with the matron of King Edward's Hospital for Officers in Grosvenor Crescent. By 5 May the fact that he was seriously ill with bronchitis could not be concealed and the first medical bulletin was issued. At noon next day he lit his last cigar; before midnight he was dead. He was in his sixty-ninth year.

The nations that had been denied his Coronation flocked to his funeral; in all 70 were represented. There were nine Kings, five Heirs Apparent, three Queens Regnant and four Dowagers. Ex-President Theodore Roosevelt represented the United States. First in precedence was the German Emperor, who had so detested his late uncle; he rode beside the young King George V in the uniform of a British Field-Marshal, a rank conferred upon him by Edward after the funeral of Queen Victoria. The Emperor and three of the Kings who followed him in the procession were destined to lose their thrones. Behind them came the man whose death was to precipitate a holocaust, as well as thinning the imperial and royal ranks: the Archduke Franz Ferdinand of Austria. It was the last and greatest set-piece of a dying era. Lord Esher wrote: 'There never was such a break-up. All the old buoys which have marked the channel of our lives seem to have been swept away.' Edward's humbler subjects, who lined the streets to watch the great parade, were soon to share Lord Esher's experience, but in a more violent form. Their ranks, too, were to be decimated in the coming years, as the old order was shattered and the map of Europe was painfully redrawn.

Further Reading

Sir J. Ponsonby, *Recollections of Three Reigns*
Sir P. Magnus, *Edward VII*
P. Jullian, *Edward and the Edwardians*
V. Cowles, *Edward VII and His Circle*
T. Lang, *Darling Daisy*

II

Political Life

Three Prime Ministers presided over British politics between 1902, when Lord Salisbury retired, and the outbreak of the First World War. One was the pawky Scot, Sir Henry Campbell-Bannerman, who led the Liberal Party in its hey-day and died in 1908; the other two were A. J. Balfour and H. H. Asquith. These two statesmen were friends, although rivals in politics, and each respected the intellectual gifts of the other. In retrospect, they seem also to have shared a certain detached urbanity, as if they stood a little above the turbulent waves of political life, even when unable to command them. If Balfour may be said to have played politics in the same spirit as he played golf, it can be said of Asquith that he brought to Cabinet meetings the cool calculation that he displayed at the bridge-table. Both suffered in the exclusive, well-ordered world of golf-club and card-room the intrusion of violence and unreason. Before their startled eyes there pass across the scene termagants, crying 'Votes for Women!', and peers from the backwoods, clutching their rusty halberds. Irish Nationalists and Orangemen strike attitudes of intolerance and outside in the cold night air stand the multitude of the unwashed and underpaid, sullenly withholding their labour, until suddenly the fire indoors goes out and the larder is empty.

It was all very perplexing and disturbing, because it had been assumed, ever since the events of 1832 and 1846, that there were no political or economic problems that could not in time be diverted into the Houses of Parliament and there cut up into convenient slices by legislators. After his disastrous defeat in 1906, Balfour had a premonition, when he wrote to Lady Salisbury,

What has occurred has nothing whatever to do with any of the things we have been squabbling over the last few years. Campbell-Bannerman is a mere cork, dancing on a torrent, which he cannot control, and what is going on here is a faint echo of the same movement which has produced massacres in St Petersburg, riots in Vienna, and Socialist processions in Berlin.

In London things were about to get worse; the representatives of the people were to be forcibly reminded that the reforms of 1832 and subsequent years had been incomplete and that they actually represented little more than half the people —all of them males. Moreover, the Upper House, which before 1846 and the repeal of the Corn Laws could claim to represent economic power rooted in the soil, had become little more than an obstinate survival. George Sturt was a lover of the country and its traditions, but in 1912 he confided to his diary his dislike of 'the English "country gentleman" who preserves game, keeps a motor car or horse, shoots, fishes, knows about land and farming, despises the poor and hates democracy'. This type, over-represented in both Houses, was not one to which the problems of an industrial age could safely be entrusted; its resistance to change distracted Asquith, especially after 1909, from the tasks that confronted him. The recalcitrance of the Lords slowed up the process of government to a point at which the electorate began to lose faith in the Liberals' pro-

Balfour. The print is a parody of the famous Pears' soap advertisement

gramme. In the years before 1914 the foundations of the Welfare State were laid, but it was the Labour Party that completed the edifice and in our day has ousted Liberalism from the two-party system.

Campbell-Bannerman and Asquith may, indeed, have been mere corks on the torrent, but the revolution that they accomplished deserves none the less to be remembered. For it was as much a revolution in the minds and hearts of the propertied class as it was a legislative revolution. Reluctantly, but irrevocably, moneyed men came to accept the principle on which all modern administration is based, namely that a part of private wealth must be taken away not merely to meet the cost of government and its Armed Forces, but to ensure that the deprived sector of the community may receive what is necessary for its well-being. Elementary as this political wisdom may seem today, it was painfully acquired in the Edwardian era. The evolutionary tradition proved itself sufficiently well embedded in the British political consciousness to ensure that the doctrines of Marx and Lenin, to whom London had been hospitable, found only a minor echo even in her slums; but it was a near-run thing.

At the end of the nineteenth century it seemed as if the Liberal Party was about to launch itself successfully upon the economic and social wave of the future. The Newcastle Programme of 1892 was full of promise and Harcourt's enactment of death duties in 1894 was an important move towards the transfer of surplus wealth from the few to the many. An observer as well qualified as Ben Tillett has recorded in his *Memories and Reflections*:

It is curious, looking back at the course of politics since the opening of the present century, to realise that in the closing decades of the last century, the Liberal Party might have secured control of the infant political movement of the workers. Schnadhorst, the great organiser and party manager of the Liberals, strove to bring this about. He declared that working-men candidates would wherever possible receive the support of his electoral association. He insisted that the

23

Keir Hardie, Mrs Bernard Shaw, Geoffrey Ramsay, and Bernard Shaw at Merthyr during the General Election of 1910

difficulties attending the question of Labour representation, grave as they were, did not arise from the attitude of the Liberal Party. Mainly they were caused by the local Liberal Associations, which whenever a Labour candidate was put forward raised objections, usually quite snobbish ones, though Schnadhorst did not say so.

The condescension shown by some Liberals was matched by the cap-in-hand diffidence of the traditionalists in the trade union movement, whose first strength was in the craft unions of skilled workers and artisans. Their leaders were mostly on the side of the existing social order, though with modifications; some of them were frankly sceptical about the efforts of Tom Mann and Tillett to organize unskilled workers. The older men believed that political wisdom resided in the two-party structure and that the Lib-Lab badge was all that a working man could hope for. In 1892, when Tillett was invited to be a candidate in both the Eastern and Western Divisions of Bradford and accepted one offer on a socialist ticket, the Labour organizers in the other Division sent an invitation to George Bernard Shaw. He declined, with the shrewd observation that there would never be a genuine Labour Party in Parliament until the workers learned to trust one another, instead of running after tall hats and frock-coats. Gradually the views of the 'New Unionism' began to prevail over those of the 'Old Guard' and in 1899 the TUC agreed to instruct its Parliamentary Committee to invite the socialists, Co-operatives, H. M. Hyndman's Social-Democratic Federation, the Fabians and other organizations to attend a Conference on Labour Representation,

24

which duly took place in the following year. The result was the creation of the Labour Representation Committee with Ramsay MacDonald as its first Secretary.

In the moulding of opinion, both inside the Labour movement and outside it, an important role was played by the Fabians, who prized the written and spoken word as more effective than the elaboration of a party organization. From the date of its foundation in 1884 the Society was able to enlist the services of some of the most skilful propagandists of the day, among them Sidney and Beatrice Webb, Edward Pease and George Bernard Shaw. Pamphlets on controversial issues flowed from them. According to G. D. H. Cole, 'The most successful of all these smaller Fabian publications was H. G. Wells' famous tract *This Misery of Boots*.' In other respects, however, Wells was far from being a model member of the Society; its moral standards were broadly those of the Nonconformists, who formed the majority of its adherents; but this was an area in which Wells conspicuously failed to conform. He informed one meeting: 'I no more regard the institution of marriage as a permanent thing than I regard a state of competitive industrialism as a permanent thing. . . .' Most Fabians would have preferred to leave marriage alone and stick to debates about industrialism. Sidney Webb developed a dislike of Wells.

Worse was to follow when Wells, who had recently published *A Modern Utopia*, tried to identify the Society with his Samurai, or ideal governing caste. Many years after he wrote:

I envisaged that reconditioned Fabian Society as becoming, by means of vigorous propaganda, mainly carried on by young people, the directive element of a reorganized socialist party. We would attack the coming generation at the high school, technical college and

Sidney and Beatrice Webb working at their home in Grosvenor Road

25

H. G. Wells

university stage, and our organization would quicken into a constructive social stratum. The idea was as good as the attempt to realize it was futile. . . . The order of the Fabian Samurai perished unborn.

The Society pursued its more mundane course and in *Ann Veronica* Wells pokes gentle fun at it. ' "It's THE society", said Miss Miniver. "It's the centre of the intellectuals. Some of the meetings are wonderful! Such earnest, beautiful women! Such deep-browed men! . . . And to think that there they are making history! There they are putting together the plans of a new world." '

The irony of the novelist contains only a small element of exaggeration. The Fabians' plans really were at the core of the new world that was coming into being. Sidney Webb had already influenced the Newcastle Programme; his disciples were in the thick of the struggle for social legislation when the Liberals returned to power in 1906. The best known of them today is William (later Lord) Beveridge.

My youthful alliance with the Webbs had achieved its purpose when it landed labour exchanges and me in the Board of Trade. Adoption of compulsory insurance meant a parting of the ways between us. The Webbs disliked social insurance as such; Lloyd George's first broaching of his scheme to them in October 1908, as reported by Beatrice, led to 'heated discussion'. . . . Sidney expressed to me his sorrow that we seemed to be doing just the opposite of what he desired. He wanted compulsory labour exchanges and voluntary insurance. . . . More than thirty years later, though still within the lifetime of the Webbs, I was to present social insurance in a new light, as an application of the Webbs' own doctrine of a national minimum for all. . . . The Beveridge Report of 1942 stemmed from what all of us had imbibed from the Webbs.

The wisdom of the decision to seek direct representation of union interests in Parliament was seen in 1901, when a judicial decision in the Taff Vale case exposed unions to claims for loss attributable to strike action. Even after the Liberals came to power and passed the Trade Disputes Act, which protected unions' funds, the need remained for legislation conceived in the interests of the unions, as such, as well as social measures benefiting the individual members. In 1909, W. V. Osborne, a member of the Amalgamated Society of Railway Servants, secured a judgment in the House of Lords inhibiting unions from using their funds to finance Labour candidates. The problem that immediately confronted the Labour Party was partly solved in 1911, when Members of Parliament, hitherto unpaid, were awarded salaries of £400 a year; but it was not until 1913 that legislation was enacted annulling the Osborne case. By that date trade union membership had risen to four million.

Whilst the success of the Labour Party in 1906 in sending 29 representatives (plus 14 miners' representatives) to Westminster was due in part to electoral alliances with the Liberals, it was widely recognized that the new party would be fully able to stand on its own legs in future. Balfour described the election results as inaugurating a new era, and Joseph Chamberlain

The Labour Party 1906

wrote of 'the labour earthquake'. The *Daily Mail* invited Philip Snowden, one of the new Members, to contribute an article on the party's aims. Commenting on the socialist programme of nationalization, the editor remarked in the same issue that the defeat of the Unionists was, in effect, 'a vast socialist upheaval disguised as a Liberal victory'. *The Annual Report of the Labour Representation Committee* proudly stated: 'Suddenly politicians of all parties realise that a new factor in politics has appeared; that organised labour as a political force is already a menace to the easy-going gentlemen of the old school, who have slumbered for so long on the green benches of St Stephens.'

Lord Knollys, King Edward's Private Secretary, was unenthusiastic: 'The old idea that the House of Commons was an assemblage of gentlemen has quite passed away.' On the other hand, one of the policemen on duty at the House, recognizing Snowden, expressed his opinion that the advent of Labour at Westminster was overdue. When Snowden slyly hinted that before long the police might have to eject some of the new Members, the policeman reconciled his duty with his political sympathies by saying, 'Oh well, sir, if it comes to that, you will find that we shall carry you out very gently!' Two years later *Punch* depicts an honest bourgeois saying to a working man: 'But, my good man, if these changes were carried out, it would mean a tremendous social upheaval.' To which the worker replies, 'Demme, I'd risk it!' He had little enough to lose.

On the surface it all seemed very English and evolutionary; but the pressure of misery was mounting, as wages failed to rise level with the cost of living. In the years between Edward's death and the outbreak of the Great War a series of paralyzing strikes occurred in an atmosphere of bitterness. The Welsh miners turned out 30,000 strong in November 1910 and at Tonypandy the troops were called in. When the dockers struck in the summer of 1911, they were demanding 8*d* an hour for a working day (or night) of ten hours; the miners struck in the following year for five shillings a shift. It sounds moderate enough today, but many employers believed they were victims of industrial blackmail and that Britain would be ruined.

Working-class resentment was matched by the acute apprehension of the gentry. George Sturt, the Farnham wheelwright, records in his diary in June 1907:

And, of late, too, class feeling has increased—since the Liberal Government took office. . . . The

Strikers stopping a wagon near Tower Bridge during the Dock Strike of 1911

rich seem absurdly frightened, but their fear, making reactionaries of them, is tending to produce just what they dread. Charles Young reports that a retired Colonel has been heard saying, 'We shall see the guillotine set up in Trafalgar Square yet'.

During the miners' strike the suggestion that the Territorial Army be used to protect 'blacklegs' was rejected partly on the ground that the newly formed units could not be trusted not to show their sympathy with the strikers. Crowsley, a Railwayman, and his printers, were jailed for the pamphlet *Don't Shoot* addressed to the soldiers.

These were not men striking over a jurisdictional dispute between unions, or the duration of a tea-break; the strikers were men driven by anxiety about food for their wives and children. Mrs Charles Masterman recorded in February 1910 a conversation between Winston Churchill, who was defending the social order, and Lloyd George, who held that it must be changed. The latter concluded the discussion by saying,

Listen. There were 600 men turned off by the G.W. [Great Western Railway] works last week. These men had to go out into the street to starve. There is not a man in that works who does not live in terror of the day when his turn will come to go. Well, I am against a social order that admits that kind of thing.

Early in the reign of Victoria, Disraeli had given dramatic expression in *Sybil* to the division of England into two 'nations' —the rich and the poor.

Two nations between whom there is no intercourse and no sympathy; who are as ignorant of each other's habits, thoughts and feelings, as if they were dwellers in different zones or inhabitants of different planets; who are formed by a different breeding, are fed by a different food, are ordered by different manners, and are not governed by the same laws.

In the reign of Edward the disparity had not changed; but a majority of the English people had begun to concern themselves with it and had elected a government to evolve practical measures to bridge the gulf between the poor and the rich. The Conservative-Unionists, however, sided with the minority and became the party of inertia and defence of the established order. Disraeli had been no believer in democracy, but the ideal of a landed aristocracy, for which he stood, implied the protection of landless men against the full rigour of supposedly immutable economic laws. His concept of *noblesse oblige* may have been a romantic one, but it was at least one that embraced the whole community. After his death his party, in spite of an infusion of new blood with Joseph Chamberlain in 1895, ceased to offer an alternative choice to people whom it had helped to enfranchize. As Lord Henry Bentinck wrote in *Tory Democracy*, the party

. . . gradually lost its national character and fell under the influence of sectional interests. The confidence of the working man was alienated, and turned into suspicion, first of the influence of the Church in education, then of the South African and afterwards of the British capitalist. The Tory Party lost the confidence of the people on the day when it

laid itself open to the
suspicion that it was
engaged in a capi-
talist conspiracy. . . .

Lord Salisbury had
flourished on the heights
of Imperialism and the
disunity of his political
opponents. The Union-
ists (as they were called
after Chamberlain's ad-
herence) turned the
century flushed with
their victory in the
'Khaki Election', in
which Chamberlain was
alleged to have assured
the voters that 'Every

Chamberlain speaking at Bingley Hall, Birmingham, 1904

seat lost to the Government is a seat gained by the Boers.'
Conservative politicians have often excelled at claiming for
themselves a monopoly of patriotism; but this time it was too
good to last. When the war was over and Balfour had succeeded his uncle as Prime Minister and leader of the party,
the split in the Liberal Party was healed. It was the Unionist
Party that began to fall apart.

The schism occurred on the issue of a protective tariff, which
had split the Tories nearly 60 years earlier, when Peel repealed
the Corn Laws. In Edward's time, as earlier, the price of the
poor man's food was the agonizing question; it brought to an
end nearly ten years of Unionist government. Margot Asquith
has recounted the prelude in her diary:

On the morning of the 16 May 1903 my husband came
into my bedroom at 20 Cavendish Square with *The Times*
in his hand. 'Wonderful news today', he said. 'And it
is only a question of time when we shall sweep the
country.' Sitting upon my bed he showed me the report

31

The young Winston Churchill speaking in the Commons

of a speech made at Birmingham the night before by Mr Chamberlain.

Chamberlain believed that imperial preference would prove to be the cement of the Empire, even if it was the solvent of his party. Balfour was not much opposed in principle to tariffs, but he agreed with the King that the people would not stand for a tax on imported foodstuff. The Prime Minister's resistance to Chamberlain, however, was not vigorous enough to hold the convinced Free Traders in his Cabinet and he lost the Duke of Devonshire as well as Chamberlain. In 1904 he also forfeited the allegiance of Winston Churchill, who in the following year moved in the House a Private Member's motion that 'This House is against Protective Taxes on food as not promoting the unity of the Empire.' The motion was not carried, but it was one of a series of damaging attacks by the young orator upon his former chief.

By the time Balfour came to the conclusion that he could not carry on, his government had managed to alienate large sections of the community. He had offended the Non-conformists, especially in Wales, by the Education Act of 1902; trade unionists resented his failure to undo by legislation the effect of the Taff Vale judgment; many people disapproved of the importation of cheap Asiatic labour into the mines of the Transvaal. The Unionists had not expected to win the election; but they quite failed to foresee the severity of the defeat awaiting them. In the last days of 1905 Lord Hugh Cecil in a letter to Margot Asquith estimated that the Liberals would have a majority of 40 over the Unionists and Irish Nationalists together; but when the votes were counted, the Liberals found they had a lead of 84 over all other parties, among which the Irish Nationalists and Labour were on most issues their potential allies. Balfour and all but 157 of his supporters lost their seats. Mrs Asquith confided to her diary: 'It certainly looks as if it were the end of the great Tory party as we have known it.' The Tories, however, had a second line of defence; beaten at the polls, they transferred the battleground to the hereditary House of Peers.

The new Prime Minister, Campbell-Bannerman, assembling around him a formidable array of talent, proceeded to introduce the reforms demanded by his followers. After gratifying organized labour by passing the Trade Disputes Act, he brought in an Education Bill providing for non-denominational religious teaching in the schools set up by the Act of 1902. Augustine Birrell, as President of the Board of Education, did not have a smooth passage; he complained that he was attacked on one flank by Sacramentalists, who regarded Bible-reading as

33

insufficient, and on the other by Secu-
larists, who were at heart against all
religious teaching. When the Lower
House finally adopted the Bill, Birrell
was frustrated in the Upper by a com-
bination of bishops and other noble
defenders of the established faith. 'The
loss of the Bill', Birrell later wrote, 'was
a great affront to the Party, which saw
itself flouted by the other House from
the start. . . .'

John Burns began to talk of abolishing the Lords and Lloyd George demanded of an audience at Oxford,
'whether this country is to be governed
by the King and his peers, or by the
King and his people'. Edward, whose
sympathies lay with his bishops, resented this attempt to bring his name
into the controversy. He disliked even
more the prospect of a clash between
the two Houses, but his efforts to bring
the two contestants to conciliate their
differences ended in failure.

Two years later, when Campbell-
Bannerman was dead and Asquith had
replaced him as Prime Minister, the
Lords threw out another Bill, the Licensing Bill, which was dear to the Non-
conformists and the apostles of temperance. It was expected that the Bill
would result in some reduction in the
consumption of alcohol and *Punch* por-
trayed an encounter in a bar between
two old topers. One says, 'Does he want
to stop our beer?' To which the other
replies, 'Not likely. If he do, 'ow's 'e
goin' to get the money for our old age

Lloyd George

34

pensions?' The peers who rejected the
Bill were more interested in barley,
hops and malt than in Mr Asquith's
fiscal problem. Their action provoked
another outburst from the Liberals,
including a remarkable comment attri-
buted by Mrs Charles Masterman to
Winston Churchill. 'I was next Winston.
He was perfectly furious at the rejection
of the Licensing Bill by the Lords,
would hardly speak; murmured peror-
ations about "the heart of every Band
of Hope in this country sinking within
them". We shall send them up such a
Budget in June as shall terrify them,
they have started the class war, they
had better be careful.'

The author of the terrifying Budget
of 1909 was Lloyd George, now Chancellor of the Exchequer, in spite of
Edward's mistrust of him. His 'People's
Budget' aimed to raise £15 million by
new taxation; tax on unearned income
was fixed at 1s. 2d. in the pound; super-
tax was imposed at 6d. in the pound on
the amount by which incomes of £5,000
and above exceeded £3,000, and land
was to be valued, so that taxation could
be levied on unearned increment from
the rising value of real estate. Strange
as it may seem today, it was this Budget that was described by Sir Edward
Carson as 'the beginning of the end of
all rights of property'. It did not im-
poverish the upper class; in 1913 a
bachelor with an annual income of
£10,000 a year, still received £9,242
after payment of tax. Although much

*Asquith. Spy cartoon from
Vanity Fair*

of the new revenue was needed to finance social benefits, part of it was for national defence. There was growing anxiety in the country, fanned by the Northcliffe Press, about the closing of what today we should call 'the Dreadnought Gap' with Germany. In this area the Unionists, so far from demanding economies, were urging Asquith to build more great battle-cruisers:

We want eight!
And we won't wait!

The expenditure on social services was what upset Northcliffe, who was all in favour of more dreadnoughts. He expressed vigorous opposition: 'The Liberal Socialist theory of taxation is that one million citizens are to serve as milch cows of the rest of the community.' It does not seem such a strange theory now; but it was anathema to most of the one million in 1909. Worst of all in the eyes of most of them was the Land Tax, which was put forward by the Chancellor of the Exchequer with the uncompromising slogan 'The land belongs to the people!' The King informed Lloyd George that he regretted attempts 'to inflame the passions of the working and lower orders against people who happen to be owners of property'. He already saw himself faced with the danger that the Lords for the first time for more than two centuries would reject a Budget sent to them by the Commons and thus precipitate a constitutional crisis. Edward, wishing at all cost to avoid such a crisis, suggested to Balfour and Lord Lansdowne that they should use their influence to induce the Lords to pass the offending Finance Bill. Whether the efforts of the Unionist leaders would have succeeded is unsure; in any case they made no attempt at persuasion. In late November the backwoodsmen converged upon Westminster. Mrs Asquith eyed them with foreboding: 'Aged peers came from remote regions of the countryside who could not even find their way to the Houses of Parliament.' The atmosphere of the Upper House during the debate was unusually tense. Lord Willoughby de Broke, who campaigned actively for rejection, wrote later, 'The peers came as near to cheering as peers can.' On 30 November 1909, the Bill was rejected by a majority of 225 and three days later Parliament was dissolved. The Liberals could hardly have had a better issue on which to go to the country. Parliamentary government could not survive if the Unionists could get their own way, whether in power or out. The Liberals saw their programme of social change paralyzed by an hereditary body in the interest of the Opposition Party, which had been overwhelmingly defeated at the polls less than four years earlier. The election slogan, 'Peers against People!' should have been fully effective. There were misgivings, however, even among staunch Liberals. Sir Edward Grey wrote to Mrs Asquith, '. . . in this country they move slowly and distrust rhetoric'. He was proved right; the innate conservatism of the British people has never shown itself more clearly. There was reluctance, especially in country districts, to abandon the traditional allegiance to the governing class. Lord Willoughby de Broke, who was more at home on a horse than on a political platform, encountered respectful audiences wherever he went. Moreover, the alternative leadership offered by some of the Liberals did not appeal to everyone, even in sections of the community that had benefited from recent reforms. Lord Harcourt wrote to Asquith: 'I found all over the country that all Lloyd George's speeches and Winston's earlier ones (not the Lancashire campaign) had done us much harm, even with the advanced men of the lower middle class.' The conviction that society was, and should be, stratified and that government was the business of the upper strata took a long time to die. In the Edwardian era it still had a good deal of life in it. It was the incompetence displayed by the ruling caste in the Great War that knocked much of the stuffing out of the myth and moved Britain closer to the Napoleonic concept of public and political service as a career open to all talents.

In another aspect the middle-class electorate proved more sophisticated than the Liberal leaders had assumed, when they based their campaign on the simple antithesis between the power of privilege and the divine right of numerical superiority. The contest was not, in fact, fought on a single issue. *Punch* (then following the middle of the road) pictured the dilemma of a Perplexed Patriot:

37

He dislikes much of the Budget, yet hates Tariff Reform; is strongly in favour of a Second Chamber, yet is infuriated by the partisan action of the House of Lords in recent years; has great faith in Mr Asquith, Sir Edward Grey, John Burns and others of the Ministry, yet non-contributory Old Age Pensions and all pandering to the Extreme Labour Party make him dreadfully unwell; mistrusts Home Rule (when conceded to people with a record like that of the present Irish Party), yet realises the astounding success of Liberal Party Policy in South Africa.

No, it was not as easy a decision as it looks 60 years later.

Although Asquith was returned to power in January 1910, he held a lead of only two votes over the Unionists; the Labour vote increased; but the real beneficiaries were the 82 Irish Nationalists, on whose favours the new Liberal Government became largely dependent. Asquith introduced a new Parliament Bill and reintroduced his former Finance Bill; the fact that the latter included a tax on Irish whiskey complicated relations with his allies. The objective of the Irish Members was to destroy the power of the Lords, in order to pave the way for the passage of an Irish Home Rule Bill. They chafed at Asquith's disinclination to press the King immediately to commit himself to the creation of peers. The Prime Minister's cautious attitude was justified by the touchiness of the King on all matters affecting his prerogative and the somewhat hesitant mandate conferred on the Government by the voters; but the delay exasperated the Irish Members, whose supporters were already beginning to listen to the advocates of violent remedies for their grievances. They learned with disgust that the Prime Minister had committed himself to the King to hold yet another election on the terms of the Parliament Bill, after it had passed the House of Commons; it was to be as close to a popular referendum as British constitutional practice would tolerate.

Death spared Edward a painful decision. Asquith was too scrupulous and too prudent to confront George V with an immediate demand for action and the summer and autumn were devoted to ineffectual conferences between the opposing forces. The electoral referendum took place in December and confirmed the previous result. The last phase of the prolonged crisis came in the summer of 1911. In July Asquith drove in an open car through a cheering crowd to the House of Commons and there let it be clearly understood for the first time that the King had agreed to create peerages. The 'last-ditchers' in the House provoked a futile uproar, which shocked at least one Labour Member, who might have believed he was sitting among his betters. Will

Ben Tillett, 'the dictator of Tower Hill', addressing the dock strikers, 1911

Crooks observed of Lord Hugh Cecil: 'Many a man has been certified insane for less than the noble Lord has done this afternoon.' In August the Lords, by the narrow margin of 17 votes, moved grudgingly into the twentieth century. Among those who would otherwise have been offered peerages were Sir Abe Bailey, J. M. Barrie, Sir Walter Gilbey, Thomas Hardy, Sir Thomas Lipton, R. C. Lehmann (editor of *Punch*), Gilbert Murray and Bertrand Russell. The Prime Minister's daughter (later Lady Violet Bonham Carter) after watching the jubilation of the Liberals, walked back to Downing Street. 'The night was breathless. . . . There was wild cheering in the streets.'

Yes, there was cheering; yet the remarkable feature of the whole episode is that it stirred the British people so lightly. It had been, after all, the greatest constitutional crisis since 1832. In that year there had been riots and the fickle crowd had broken the Duke of Wellington's windows. In 1867, when Parliament was deadlocked on the question of extending the suffrage, there had been mass demonstrations and rioting in Hyde Park. Yet in 1910, when Asquith twice sought the support of an electorate, whose will had been frustrated by an hereditary House, popular opinion failed to catch fire; indeed by the end of the year many people seemed bored by the whole controversy. The fact is that the large segment of society to which reform was most vital (the Irish apart) did not put the ballot-box first in their priorities. The more aggressive of the trade union leaders had seen already that action through constitutional procedures was not enough. In 1890 Ben Tillett and Tom Mann collaborated in a pamphlet which put their attitude very concisely.

> The statement that the new Trade Unionists look to Government and legislation is bunkum. The keynote is to organise first and take action in the most effective way as soon as organisation warrants action, instead of specially looking to Government. The lesson is being thoroughly well taught and learned that we must look to ourselves alone, though this, of course, does not preclude us from exercising our rights of citizenship.

The apostles of Direct Action were not primarily interested in getting candidates elected, nor were they primarily interested in what went on in Parliament; they were interested in exerting power to remedy industrial abuses which had gone on too long; they had no time for the slow-moving political drama played at Westminster by actors who for the most part had upper-class accents and attitudes. Even the TUC was insufficiently belligerent for Tom Mann, who criticized it openly at a Conference in 1910 of the Industrial Syndicalist Education League.

In January 1906 Balfour wrote to Austen Chamberlain: '. . . it is quite obvious . . . that we are dealing with forces not called into being by any of the subjects about which Parties have been recently squabbling, but rather due to a general movement of which we see more violent manifestations in Continental politics. . . .' Balfour was right, and if he had chosen to give a name to the continental movement it would have been Syndicalism. The spearhead in Britain was provided by the transport workers. Tillett, who led the Dock, Wharf, Riverside and General Workers' Union, was instrumental in creating the National Transport Workers' Federation, which after the First World War became the mammoth Transport and General Workers' Union. The Federation, which with the new National Union of Railwaymen and National Union

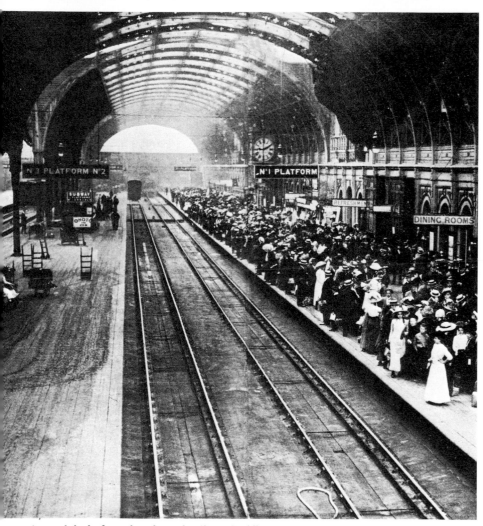

A crowded platform, but deserted rails at Paddington Station during the railway strike, 1911

of Mineworkers played the leading part in the industrial upheavals of 1910–11, had a well-defined strategic objective. Transport was the life-blood of the country and, if it was brought to a halt, urban life would grind to a standstill.

So it proved. As a result of the strike of transport workers, London was brought to within measurable distance of a food famine.

Everywhere the docks were at a standstill and the transport ceased to move. Pickets were unnecessary, because there were no workers to be found willing to blackleg upon their fellows. The great markets of the City were idle; the rush and turmoil of the City's traffic congesting the principal ways dwindling to a little trickle as motor buses, motor-cars and private vehicles of all kinds felt the pressure of a shortage of petrol, and all the immense volume of trading traffic through the City streets from the docks to the warehouses and the great railway terminals ceased to move; whilst all down the river only the tide moved, and on the wharves tons of fruit and vegetable, and great accumulations of merchandise lay neglected and untouched. . . . Coal and water, gas and electricity, meat, flour, ice and vegetables, all the materials of commerce, products of the workshop and factory and the mill, borne on the railway or transported by road, canal and river, arrested in their movements.

It had taken over a century, but now the wheel of the Industrial Revolution had completed its circle: those who produced the wealth that had built the cities, with their fine public buildings and their infamous slums, had at length realized that what they had given they had also the power to take away.

Further Reading

R. C. K. Ensor, *England (1870–1914)*
G. Dangerfield, *The Strange Death of Liberal England*
R. S. Churchill, *Winston S. Churchill* (Volumes I and II)
R. Jenkins, *Mr Balfour's Poodle*
R. Jenkins, *Asquith*
M. Asquith, *Autobiography*
A. J. Young, *Balfour*
Lord Snowden, *An Autobiography* (Volume I)
B. Tillett, *Memories and Reflections*

III

Life in Towns

At the turn of the century Britain was still governed, in the main, by men who derived their importance from ownership of land and the traditions of a landed aristocracy dominated society. The wealth of the nation, however, came chiefly from trade and industry and the British had become an urban people. The census of 1901 recorded that above 25 millions lived in towns, 4½ million of them in London; only 7½ millions lived elsewhere. By 1911 41 per cent of the population of England and Wales were concentrated in London, South-East Lancashire, Merseyside, the West Midlands, West Yorkshire and Tyneside. In the 'dark, Satanic mills' of these industrial areas was produced the great bulk of the wealth which was invested in all parts of the world and paid for the raw materials for the factories and the imported food for the labouring masses. Industrialism had come to stay; but much of the optimism, which in Victorian times had greeted the age of mass production, was fading. Max Beerbohm expressed the misgivings in his cartoon depicting Industrial System addressing Civilization: 'No, my dear, you may have ceased to love me; but you took me for better or wuss in younger and 'appier days, and there'll be no getting away for you from me, ever.'

The population had been increasing year by year since the first census of 1801. In the nineteenth century we were a young people; in 1901 42·5 per cent of the population was between the ages of one and 19. The Edwardian decade saw the beginning of a change; in 1911 the percentage increase of the population, measured against the preceding decade, fell below

11 per cent for the first time on record. The birth rate turned downward during the same period; the death rate also declined. As a people the British were ageing. The pressure of population on available resources was high and emigration, which reached its peak (268,485) in 1912, was to some extent a safety-valve. Although new industries were sprouting during the Edwardian period, unemployment was a constant threat to the worker. The available figures, which are from trade unions, show average unemployment of 4½ per cent from 1901 to 1913, with a peak of 7·8 per cent in 1908, but it must be kept in mind that in 1909 trade union membership was still below 2½ million and total unemployment may well have been substantially greater than these percentages suggest.

Before we investigate how this urban multitude lived, let us look briefly at the distribution of national wealth. In 1901 only 400,000 out of a population of 32·5 million earned more than £400 a year. Income tax, which after the Boer War fell again to 1s. in the pound, began with incomes of £160 a year, but less than one million citizens were liable. It will be clear from the bare recital of these figures that Britain suffered from a serious maldistribution of the national income, or—to put it more exactly—the majority suffered and a small minority benefited.

Men waiting for work outside a London builder's

It was a minority which had abandoned all scruple about displaying its riches. The new King had had the chandeliers cleaned at Buckingham Palace, where they had been blackened by gas, and beneath them the great ladies of society were on show, 'encrusted with diamonds and decked with flowers' (as E. F. Benson said of the Duchess of Devonshire). On one royal occasion, Daisy, Princess of Pless, wore a dress of gold tissue with a gold train costing £400. Asprey's and Cartier's supplied them with precious stones and trinkets, Sargent painted

Alice Keppel

their portraits. American millionaires, merchant princes and City magnates, admitted by Edward's indulgence to the highest circle, jostled the landed aristocracy and drove up the cost of staying in the race. Sir Ernest Cassel imported 800 tons of Carrara marble to decorate his house in Park Lane and employed Duveen to furnish its walls with masterpieces of art.

Let us look at this way of life, as it begins, through the eyes of Sonia, daughter of Alice Keppel, the Edwardian beauty, who was the King's confidante. She was born in Portman Square two weeks after the relief of Mafeking and describes how 'on the day of my birth, Papa, and other anxious friends, smothered the road outside our house with straw, whereby to deaden the sound of traffic.' When the ordeal of childbirth was safely over, tribute was paid to Alice, the mother-goddess. 'I can see the flowers sent as oblations to this goddess, the orchids, the malmaisons, the lilies. Great beribboned baskets of them, delivered in horse-drawn vans by a coachman and attendant in livery. They would have been banked in tall, cut-glass vases about her bed.'

The pleasant lives of the rich were not, of course, confined to London. 'Christmas was spent at Crichel, Lord and Lady Alington's country house; New Year was spent at Melbury, where lived Lord and Lady Ilchester; Easter was spent at Biarritz, and

45

the summer holidays were spent at Duntreath Castle in Stirling-shire, Uncle Archie Edmondstone's and Mamma's old home.' In the spring there was a reverse flow into London of wealthy families who owed it to themselves to see and be seen during the London season; those with marriageable daughters were especi-ally faithful in their observance of this social pilgrimage. If they did not own a London house, they would take one furnished for the season, bringing linen, plate and carriage horses with them. Four or more tons of luggage would be conveyed to the station nearest to their country seat and the station-master in a top hat would see the head of the family and his lady into the train.

A great retinue of servants would accompany them and, as 'country cousins', join the innumerable attendants upon those who made London their normal place of residence. Little Sonia Keppel, for example, was tended in infancy by a nurse, who in turn was served by a nurse-maid. Below stairs, the needs of the household were supervised by Mr Rolfe, the butler, and Mrs Wright, the cook, supported by Miss Draper, Peggie, Katie and George, the boot-boy. Failure to employ at least one footman, on which experienced butlers usually insisted, is explained by Miss Keppel as due to the fact that money was a commodity 'which, at this time, neither my mother nor my

Menservants in the early 1900s

A fashion plate showing two contrasting styles of dress

father possessed in great measure'. So numerous were the male attendants of the élite of Mayfair that they boasted their own favourite public house, 'The Running Footman' in Hay's Mews. There the gentleman's gentleman, his status carefully adjusted according to the wealth and title of his master, would discuss with his social equals the weather, the Turf, the prospects of retirement—everything except the confidential gossip of the great house in which he served.

By day the man of fashion was never seen—after his ride in Rotten Row—except in his frock-coat and top hat of pearl-grey, carrying a stick and gloves. His lady would have an

47

enormous hat on top of her padded hair-style and would be bedizened with ribbons, feather boa and parasol. If she rode, she rode side-saddle. Women's fashions were still created in London; it was the exception to have a gown made by a Paris dressmaker until Mrs Asquith invited Monsieur Paul Poiret to display his creations at No. 10 Downing Street. The styles of the smart set were copied by home dressmakers, using the sewing-machines which had come into general use in the Victorian period. The coat-and-skirt had become the wear not only of the new 'career-woman', but also of the upper class; tweeds gradually replaced the silk costume. Although all skirts were, by our standards, very long, fashion decreed some variation in them, as well as in sleeves. *Punch* took note of this in a verse of the autumn of 1904:

> *Time was, not very long ago,*
> *When Mabel's walking skirt*
> *Trailed half-a-yard behind to show*
> *How well she swept the dirt.*
> *But 'short and sweet' are in again;*
> *No more the grievance rankles,*
> *For Mabel's now curtailed her train*
> *And shows her dainty ankles.*
>
> *But Mabel has a thrifty mind,*
> *To supplement her charms,*
> *The frills that once she wore behind*
> *She fastens on her arms.*
> *Her sleeves are made in open bags*
> *Like trousers in the Navy.*
> *No more she sweeps the street, but drags*
> *Her sleeve across the gravy.*

One of the conspicuous differences between the Edwardian man in the street and his descendant today is that the former would never have been seen out of doors without a hat; even the very poor wore hats if they could possibly afford it. To go bareheaded was to show deference to all whom one encountered. For the man about town it was essential to have the right hat for the occasion. If he was going shooting or fishing, he needed a cap of hand-woven tweed or a deerstalker; for hunting, a bowler-hat with a button and ring in the brim to attach it firmly to his person. The most popular model was the 'Coke', named after the famous Norfolk family; it cost 12s. 6d. made by the best hatters in London. The top hat was *de rigueur*, although one of Edward's dubious innovations was the Homburg, worn with a short coat. The top hat was specially styled in accordance with the whim of the season; it would cost 25s. and would last a lifetime. It never did, of course, because the hatters were too shrewd to allow the fashionable world to believe that the curly brim of last year was smart enough for this. A hatter might go in for as many as 30 subtle variations of style, shape and 'set'. Fred Willis, who was himself a hatter in the Golden Age of the hat, has recounted how the social standing of a customer could be gauged by the way in which he asked for his hat. 'If he described it as a silk hat we knew he belonged to suburbia and respectability; if he asked for a top hat he belonged to the City (Stock Exchange or Mincing Lane), but if he demanded a topper he was out of the top drawer, an Olympian. . . .' The Olympian would drop in every day to have his hat ironed, but after May was out he would appear not in his 'topper', but in a

Two extremes of society meet at Ascot

straw boater until the end of the London season. In the evening he would have his collapsible tall hat for going to Covent Garden, where in the summer of 1905 Melba and Caruso were both singing. Such was the importance of having the right hat that the well-dressed man would travel with a special leather hat-case in order to be rightly equipped for the opera, Ascot, Cowes or the moors.

Alice Keppel seems to have had an awareness, unlike so many of her contemporaries, that their world of privilege was underpinned by human misery. Her daughter recounts how Lord Alington, one of her mother's wealthy admirers, used to take her for afternoon drives in his carriage.

One rather dull day he called for her, and, as usual, asked her where he should drive her. 'Hoxton, please,' she said. Hoxton was a poor slum in East London, where Lord Alington owned a lot of property. Hitherto he had not visited it and, as can be imagined, he was not enthusiastic to do so. But Mamma insisted. From her subsequent description, the drive was funereal. Along dreary streets the horses clopped slowly, the smart equipage jeered at, or sullenly watched, by dull-eyed men and women and miserably-clad children.

'Public penury, private ostentation': C. F. G. Masterman summed it up in a Tacitean phrase. He also took part in the Liberal administrations which after 1906 tried to do something about the penury. Although the Edwardian period was not marked by depressions comparable to those which had occurred from time to time in the previous reign, the working men regarded economic conditions with misgiving. Coal was still the foundation of the economy; in 1907 the value of the coal output was twice that of the cotton industry and three and a half times that of iron and steel. New industries, such as the electrical and chemical, were coming to the fore, making fresh demands on the labour force; yet miners' wages showed a 10 per cent decline between 1900 and 1911. High percentages of workers in major industries earned 25s. a week or less; for example:

Iron and steel	31·4 per cent	Cotton	40·6 per cent
Chemicals	40·3 per cent	Railways	49·7 per cent

Of no major industry is it recorded that as many as 20 per cent of the workers earned as much as 45s. a week. The stagnation of wages would have been less serious if the cost of living had been falling, but in spite of the relative cheapness of imported foodstuffs the trend was upward. The price of the 4-lb. loaf rose only slightly from 1900 to 1911, but other wholesale prices showed an increase after 1905.

Since 1889, when the Dockers and Gasworkers had shown great militancy, unskilled workers generally had become more effectively organized and in the years up to 1914 they were narrowing the gap between themselves and the old aristocrats of labour, the skilled craftsmen, who had achieved trade union solidarity at a much earlier date. In the small, exclusive unions,

The family of a skilled worker at tea. Respectability is upheld by the biblical text, the encyclopaedia behind the glass bookcase and the stiff collars of the children

such as those of the Brushmakers and the Hatters, a man served a long apprenticeship, but once he was accepted he could be fairly sure of work, in spite of seasonal depressions, as long as his health lasted. In the bad old days, before Old Age Pensions, paid holidays and National Health and Unemployment Insurance, good health was the vital factor determining whether a worker would raise his family in modest comfort or end his days in the workhouse. Although age and misfortune might bring both the skilled and the unskilled worker to the indignity of being buried by the parish, the skilled craftsman in his prosperity had always been very conscious of the social and economic frontier separating him from the unskilled worker. In the early years of the new century this frontier was becoming blurred; the artisan, who was often conservative in his ways and Conservative in his politics, felt that his superior status was being eroded by the gains achieved by the mass unions and the earnings of semi-skilled machine-operators paid by results.

At the same time the artisans and craftsmen were dimly aware of a gap opening in the ranks above them. The old-fashioned master, who knew his men and to some extent shared the same working conditions, was disappearing. Firms were capitalizing and the new management knew all about a balance-sheet, but less about how the product was made. Company directors, owing allegiance to a remote and anonymous body of shareholders, no longer had the same understanding of the problems of their workpeople; a new army of technicians and white-collar workers was filling the gulf between master and man. Many of the tragic misunderstandings and disorders of industrial life in Britain had their genesis in this period. Production was ceasing to be a co-operative effort; it was beginning more and more to resemble a struggle between the power of the profit-maker and the stubborn and occasionally violent resistance of organized labour.

If a skilled craftsman, blessed with good health and not too many children, was earning two guineas a week, or more, he would have had no difficulty in finding a solidly built terrace house in the London area for a rent of 12s. 6d. a week. There would be five or six rooms and a scullery and, if the family was

52

small, or one of the daughters had married and left home, there would probably be room for a lodger contributing 10s. a week to the exchequer; he would share the family supper and also the midday meal on Sundays. The front room, which might contain a pianola, would only be used on special occasions. There would be no bathroom, but in the kitchen a galvanized iron bath would serve both for laundering and for the regular bath-nights of the members of the family. A mangle would probably be the only labour-saving device in the kitchen.

The houses of the skilled workers

If father had chosen well, the house would have a small garden at the back and here he would grow such vegetables as could survive the soot of London's millions of coal fires and the constant drip of mother's washing on the line. The kitchen stove would burn coal, bought at 19s. 6d. a ton; the lighting would probably come from a gas-bracket or oil-lamp. Although all the houses would look much the same, there would be life in the streets; the cries of vendors would compete with the barrel-organ which at the beginning of the period might have played 'After the Ball' and, at the end, a Franz Lehar or Strauss waltz. A knife-grinder would come by, operating his machine with a foot pedal. Instead of the boy who today comes to the door and offers to wash your car, his grandfather would have offered you a few pails of horse manure for your garden. His capital investment in this trade was not large, as plenty of horse manure could still be scavenged in the streets of London and other cities.

Wages were so low that all members of the family would take a job, even at the depressed rates paid to young boys and women. A waitress in a cheap coffee-house might work from

7 a.m. to 11 p.m. for 5s. a week plus her food. At the turn of the century, when girl telephonists began to be employed, they would start at no more than 11s. a week. An office boy, who had just left school, might earn 6s. a week by working from 9 a.m. to 7 p.m. One such was Neville Cardus, who has recorded his youth in Manchester.

> After the break up of Sumner Place, I lived precariously for a while, usually in odd jobs ranging from a messenger-boy to driver of a joiner's and carpenter's handcart. I dwelt in a single back room in a Manchester lodging, so cold in winter for want of a blanket that I collected newspapers and periodicals to pile on my bed over my feet. There were loose boards in the uncarpeted bedroom floor. . . .

In December 1904 a 'stroke of fortune' befell young Neville Cardus; he answered an advertisement in the *Manchester Evening News*: 'Wanted Smart Respectable Youth for Insurance Office. Hours 9.30 to 5.'

A knife-cleaner

> I started at 8s. a week and in the course of eight years, from 1904 to 1912, I advanced to a golden sovereign, by which time I had celebrated my 21st birthday . . . . I helped another clerk, a man of middle years, to write out the policies; the Flemings would not use the 'newfangled' typewriting machine. . . .

The telephone exchange at St Paul's churchyard

The earnings of younger members of the family provided a bulwark against the otherwise disastrous results of illness or accident suffered by the breadwinner. Although the first Workmen's Compensation Act had been passed in 1897, it was not until 1906 that the legal obligation to compensate a workman who had suffered injury was extended to include virtually all employers. Previously, even coal-mining had not been covered. Moreover, little was known about the long-term effects of work in dangerous branches of the chemical and other industries. A wife whose husband was incapacitated could defer the day of reckoning and obtain food for herself and her children only by pawning their possessions—'making up a bundle for uncle', as it was often called. That this was common practice is indicated by the count made in 1906 that there were 692 pawnshops within a radius of ten miles of the Royal Exchange, averaging 5,000 pledges of under £10 in value every month.

Although the 1911 census showed that the drift from the land had been checked, the towns had continued in the preceding decade to fill up with the less competent or less fortunate of the rural populations. The cities were unprepared to receive them. The same period marked a 15 per cent decline in building at a time when the need for new housing had never been more

55

acute. The building trade was stagnant largely because rents were not rising; but this stability was little consolation to new arrivals in cities already bursting at the seams. The houses of middle-class families, which had removed to remoter suburbia, were suffering the familiar process of subdivision for the benefit of new immigrants into the cities and respectable districts were degenerating into slums. The Housing and Town Planning Act of 1909 gave local authorities more power to pull down slum property and rebuild; but they were slow to move into a field long reserved to the landlord and entrepreneur. In 1911 8·6 per cent of the population of England and Wales was living more than two to a room. In some parts of the country the percentage was substantially higher. The London average was 16·7 per cent; in East End boroughs, such as Shoreditch, as many as 36 per cent lived more than two to a room. The

Saturday night at the pawnbroker's

figures were little better in Newcastle and Sunderland; indeed in Sunderland overcrowding was worse than it had been 20 years earlier.

Birmingham's civic motto was 'Forward', but in 1911, when the population had reached 525,000, 10 per cent of them still lived more than two to each room. There were 40,000 back-to-back houses and areas where 30 persons had to use one tap as their sole water-supply. Until 1904, when the city spent £6 million to bring water from

A family living in one room in 1912

Wales, the private suppliers only turned on the water at certain times of the day, which aggravated the lack of sanitation. There were only 300 acres of open space in the whole city and in 1911, a year in which there were 5,000 cases of tuberculosis, Bishop Gore spoke of 'a profound social discontent' in the city which was his diocese. When the young Winston Churchill first visited Manchester with his new Private Secretary, Eddie Marsh, they took a walk on the evening of their arrival and found themselves in a working-class district. 'Fancy living in one of these streets,' said Churchill to his companion, 'never seeing anything beautiful, never eating anything savoury, never saying anything clever!' It was the lot of the vast majority of the English people.

Conditions in London attracted most attention. In 1902 a young American journalist of strong socialist convictions, Jack London, went into the East End to see for himself.

Nowhere in the streets of London may one escape the sight of abject poverty, while five minutes' walk from almost any point will bring one to a slum; but the region my hansom was now penetrating was one unending slum. The streets were filled with a new and different race of people, short of stature, and of wretched or beer-sodden appearance. We rolled along through miles of brick and squalor, and from each cross street and alley flashed long vistas of brick and misery.

Once inside the doors of these sordid dwellings, conditions proved even worse than the exterior suggested. Jack London, dressed as a poor labourer, pursued his inquiries.

Not only was one room deemed sufficient for a poor man and his family, but I learned that many families occupying single rooms had so much space to spare as to be able to take a lodger or two. When such rooms can be rented from 3s. to 6s. per week, it is a fair conclusion that a lodger with a reference should obtain floor space for, say, from 18d. to a shilling. He may even be able to board with the sublettees for a few shillings more.

Multiple occupation of a room was not the whole story; in the worst areas there was multiple occupation of beds. Each successive occupant would be alloted eight hours in the 24, so that the bed was never empty.

Those living under these conditions would be still earning something, clinging, however precariously, to the outermost fringes of the economic system. Below them were the outcasts, those for whom nothing remained but the casual ward or homelessness. It was estimated that upwards of 35,000 roamed the streets all night, constantly chivvied by the law, in case sleep overcame them in a public place. Iron railings surrounded the parks to prevent those 'carrying the banner', that is, those walking the streets all night, from finding refuge there. Jack London writes:

Among those who carry the banner, Green Park has the reputation of opening its gates earlier than the other parks, and at quarter past four in the morning, I and many more

The 'penny sit-up' in the Salvation Army Shelter at Blackfriars

entered Green Park. It was raining again, but they were worn out with the night's walking, and they were down on the benches and asleep at once.

The workhouses were so hated that, in spite of the severity of the conditions outside, many avoided the workhouse for as long as their physical strength permitted. In any case long queues formed before the workhouse opened its doors and those who came late, often those who had followed the will-o'-the-wisp of a job, would find themselves turned away and forced on to the streets. As Jack London stood in the queue, it was explained to him how he would fare.

Having taken a cold bath on entering, I would be given for supper six ounces of bread and 'three parts of skilly'. 'Three parts' means three-quarters of a pint, and 'skilly' is a fluid concoction of three quarts of oatmeal stirred into three buckets and a half of hot water.

On this diet the inmates would earn their keep next day by picking oakum or breaking stones. Anyone seeking to evade his

59

quota of work risked a prison sentence. The administrators of the Poor Law were out to save the money of the virtuous and thrifty and prove to vagabonds that idleness did not pay.

The squalid, insanitary sprawl of industrial cities impressed well-to-do citizens in different ways. The great majority turned their back on the disagreeable problem and moved out. It occurred, however, to a few men of vision that it might be possible to plant a town in the country with limitations on its growth, instead of allowing existing cities gradually to erode the rural amenities. Light industry and country might, it was thought, be married, as Venice married the sea. The best-known pioneer in this field was Sir Ebenezer Howard whose book *Tomorrow* pointed the way. He founded the Garden City Association, which developed into the Town and Country Planning Association. His concept was that of forming a Trust owning the freehold of an area in which industry should be domesticated in communities of about 30,000, protected by a green belt, in which agriculture would continue to be practised. In 1903 the site on the Icknield Way was acquired for Letchworth, which was planned on a basis of 10–12 houses per acre. The State took notice. In 1909 an Act was passed authorizing Local Government Boards to devise schemes of planned

Tramps sleeping in the park

development, by which the worst excesses of speculative builders could be forestalled. It was a small, but valuable, beginning. The idea of divorcing industry from slums was not, of course, a new one. At

Cottages at Port Sunlight

the end of the 1880s Port Sunlight had been established on Merseyside with its own churches, social clubs and halls, schools and gymnasia. Above all, there were parks and allotments to encourage the workpeople, who were often recruits from the countryside, to believe that their roots were still in the soil. The Cadbury family created Bournville a few years later as a more salubrious appendage of Birmingham and here, too, gardens were a feature. The business of inducing Englishmen to live in blocks of flats is even today only partially successful. The Rowntree Village Trust, operating on the outskirts of York, dates from 1904. Keir Hardie welcomed these developments on behalf of organized labour: 'What I have to say about Bournville is that, if we could compel our local authorities to follow where private enterprise has led, we should speedily eradicate slumdom, and with slumdom many of the evils which follow in its train, especially the great white scourge, consumption.'

Unfortunately, the experiments of these paternalist employers, mainly Quakers, were not widely followed. Too many property-owners basked in the comfortable notion that poverty was a judgment of God, primarily attributable to lack of thrift and temperance, and that the character of the British working man was such that, whatever housing was provided for him, he would soon turn it into a slum. This belief, which had the merit of absolving the conscience of the rich, gave birth to the legend that, if baths were provided for the dwellings of the poor, coals would be kept in them. It was strange that so few landlords were prepared to put this myth to the test, in an age which claimed to believe that cleanliness was next to godliness.

61

As in all periods of history, those who troubled their heads about social problems were very much in the minority. Most people, faced with the manifest and manifold ills of urbanism, crossed the road and, as soon as they were able, passed by on the other side. It was, happily for them, a period in which increasing numbers of people were able to do so. Retired merchants with sound investments; leisured sons of North Country clothiers or cotton-spinners; spinsters living on a family trust; all basked in the hey-day of the *rentier*. Whilst the cost of living rose only slowly, there were many profitable openings for capital, both at home and overseas. Between 1899 and 1913 income assessed on profits and interest increased by 55 per cent. A married man with £500 a year could boast a respectable London address and employ three servants at an outlay of no more than £75 a year. With £1,000 a year he was a rich man and could keep horses and a sailing boat; the amenities of an uncongested coast and countryside were at his disposal.

It was not surprising that many people in this category left the cities for good. They retreated up the Thames valley to Bourne End and Cookham; they dotted the low hills of the Home Counties with their villas and converted farm-houses; they settled in swarms on the South Coast. H. G. Wells left his house at Woking, overlooking the railway, and built at Sandgate. 'We found an architect in C. F. A. Voysey, the pioneer in the escape from the small villa residence to the bright and comfortable pseudo-cottage.' The cost of such a move was not exorbitant; for £380 my father largely furnished in 1908 a house near the sea with five principal bedrooms and two maid's rooms.

Girls playing cricket in the grounds of the factory at Bourneville, 1909

Those whose daily work tied them to the cities could not move so far; but they looked with growing distaste on the ill-lit, ill-paved streets and the public houses, which at midnight spewed out their clientele. They yearned for the cleaner air and roadways of the suburbs, where lace curtains would not need to be washed so often; the fern, or aspidistra, on its bamboo tripod would not become coated with grime; and their children on their way to school would not run the risk of being reviled by children of the lower orders. One afternoon father would go prospecting on his bicycle, and there would be confabulations with builders or house agents. A house with garden in Balham could be bought for £850 and fully furnished for £150.

Those who moved to the inner ring of suburbs took advantage of new and rapid means of transport; travelling conditions were far superior to those enjoyed by commuters today. Towards the end of 1900 the American financier, Charles Tyson Yerkes, drove out in a hansom to Hampstead Heath, which was at first visualized as the terminus of the Hampstead Tube. Arrived there, he decided to drive on past the Bull and Bush, where a station was planned, to Golders Green, which at that date was in a rural setting and so remained for a few more years, whilst tunnelling for the Tube went on. On the opposite side of London, Clapham Common, then a select residential area, had by 1900 been linked by Tube to the City via Kennington and Stockwell. In the decade ending 1901 the population of Middlesex and Surrey showed an increase of 33 per cent. The suburbs round Birmingham acquired 60,000 new residents between 1900 and 1910. Brick, mortar and asphalt crept out over the green fields. 'The country surrounding Hanwell', wrote Charlie Chaplin, 'was beautiful in those days, with lanes of horse-chestnut trees, ripening wheatfields and heavy-laden orchards. . . .' But not for much longer.

Rents were not high; a six-room house in Clapham or Edmonton could be had for 10s.–12s. a week. Suburban dwellers were already showing a preference for distinguishing their identities by a name rather than a number. In 1904 *Punch* made fun of the outcrop of similar names, which was creating problems for postmen. In the categories between £30 to £50 a

Architect's design for a house at Wimbledon, 1909

year *Punch* assigned the names Bellevue, Fairview and Bella Vista; The Elms, The Firs, The Laurels and The Laburnums; and Rosedene, Moss Dene and Willow Dene. In the more pretentious £2 10*s.* a week bracket belonged the Holmes, Hursts, Crofts and Granges.

The suburban dwellers represented in the main the new race of men and women with some education and social pretension who regarded themselves as superior to artisans and craftsmen, and were securing a footing for themselves in the ranks of the middle class. Opportunities of white-collar employment in commerce and the public service were growing. The Civil Service was still small; the number so employed in 1914 was only 167,630, of whom no less than 123,670 worked in various capacities for the Post Office. But the demand for clerks, book-keepers and assistant managers seemed unlimited, and their daughters were able to supplement the family income as shorthand-writers and telephonists until marriage claimed them.

Jokes about the social pretensions of suburbia were commonplace at the turn of the century; we recall how George Grossmith's Mr Pooter ordered his champagne—'Jackson Frères'—from his grocer and how his made-up bow-tie fell into the pitstalls at the Tank Theatre, Islington. A few years later 'Saki' (H. H. Munro) drew an analogy in his sketch, *The Mappined Life*, between the new terraces at the Zoo, where the animals could be seen in natural surroundings, and the empty suburban routine of Mr and Mrs Gurtleberry.

'They look so spacious and natural, but I suppose a good deal of what seems natural to us would be meaningless to a wild animal.'

'That is where our superior powers of self-deception come in,' said her niece; 'we are able to live our unreal, stupid little lives on our particular Mappin terrace, and persuade ourselves that we really are untrammelled men and women leading a reasonable existence. . . . We are trammelled by restrictions of income and opportunity, and above all by lack of initiative.'

Yet suburbia also had its triumphs: Rufus Isaacs rose from Belsize Park to become Viceroy of India, surmounting the anti-Semitism of the period as an additional hazard on the way.

A society in which wealth first begins to seep through to the lower levels is notoriously an acquisitive society. The suburban trains that carried husbands to work in the cities, would carry their wives on a shopping spree a little later in the day. One of those who catered most astutely for the suburban housewife's wish to make her shopping expedition an event and an adventure

Playing the pianola

Gordon Selfridge

was Gordon Selfridge. He had learned in the great department store, Marshall Field of Chicago, how to promote the sale of a wide range of products under one roof. When he came to England in 1906, he found British methods deplorably old-fashioned; shop-windows were crammed with ill-assorted goods; inside the shop everything was stowed away in drawers; lighting and ventilation left much to be desired. He selected Oxford Street as the new Mecca of merchandising and spent £36,000 on advertising before launching his store in March 1909 with £100,000 worth of goods and a staff of 1,800. 'In my store,' he said, 'women can realise some of their dreams . . . they come here as guests, not customers to be bullied into buying. This is not a shop, it is a social centre.'

Commercial enterprise was not confined to the metropolis. One of those who decided to tempt the suburban housewife to shop nearer home was Frank Bentall, who at 24 opened his small drapery shop with an eight-yard frontage at Kingston-on-Thames. In 1900, 33 years later, he owned the biggest department store in Surrey and was expanding rapidly; by 1910 his son, Leonard, had an annual turnover of £60,000 and was employing over 100 staff. The staff worked as hard as the proprietor; normal hours were from 8 a.m. to 8 p.m.; the store closed at 2 p.m. on Wednesdays, but was open late on Saturdays. The first porter, taken on in 1907, earned 23s. a week, of which 9s. went in rent. An advertising manager was employed from 1909 and two years later a free daily delivery service was operated to many parts of Surrey and Middlesex, at first by horse-drawn van, then by motor van.

Like store-owners, Lord Northcliffe had his eye on the changing tastes of the housewife and was keen to advertise his product in novel ways. In 1908 he launched the *Daily Mail* Ideal Home Exhibition, which thereafter has presented annually the fruits of an age of increasing popular affluence. It took eight days to mount the exhibition, which was opened by the Lord Mayor of London. Much of the equipment of those days seems antiquated to us: 'dollies' for the wash-tub; gas geysers of burnished copper; circular knife-sharpening machines (there was no stainless steel). But there were glimpses of what the future held for servantless housewives. Electric fires, kettles and irons were coming into use; also washing-machines, although these used steam, heated by gas, and had to be rotated by hand. H. C. Booth's vacuum-cleaner had by 1908 been domesticated and no longer needed to be drawn by horses to the house and operated through the window.

If domestic gadgetry developed slowly in the Edwardian period, the reason is that the servant problem had scarcely begun; domestic service absorbed more labour than the metallurgical industries. In well-appointed homes, which were beginning to be

Bentalls in 1910

The 'Baby Daisy' vacuum cleaner

wired for electricity, there was a symbol of the human machinery by which they ran. In the servants' hall, butler's pantry, or in the kitchen of a more modest establishment, there was an indicator, showing each room, with a miniature shutter which fell when a bell was rung. It might be that a caller with top hat, gloves and silver-mounted cane had come to express his thanks for the previous night's dinner-party; it might be the timely delivery of another mountain of coal (for a large house might burn three-quarters of a ton a day); it might be that, four flights up, the reel of silk thread of the lady of the house had rolled under the bed; it might be the sack. In any case it was the hall-mark of a society in which it was still expected that everyone should know his place and answer his summons.

Further Reading

E. J. Hobsbawm, *Labouring Men*
Johnson, Whyman and Wykes, *A Short Economic and Social History of Twentieth-Century Britain*
A. Weymouth, *This Century of Change*
F. Willis, *A Book of London Yesterdays*
J. London, *People of the Abyss*
W. H. Davies, *Autobiography of a Super-Tramp*
Cunnington and Lucas, *Occupational Costume in England*

IV

People in Motion

The reign of Edward VII is not commonly regarded as a revolutionary period, yet in the field of transportation the adjective can properly be applied. It was the age in which electrical propulsion was generally recognized as an alternative to steam; in which man took to the air, and in which the submarine became an instrument of European warfare and dreadnoughts were powered with turbine engines. Above all, it was the age in which the petrol-driven motor car was grafted on to people's lives, not merely as the rich man's plaything, but as a normal means of public and private conveyance. Today, when we struggle as best we may with the backlash of this last-mentioned revolution, we can too easily forget what joy it was for the motorist in that first dawn to be alive.

It was, of course, no sudden dawn. The principle of the internal combustion engine had long been known to Victorian technology: but the Red Flag Act, and the mentality behind its provisions and the amendments adopted in 1878, had inhibited development of mechanically propelled vehicles. Moreover, the British aristocracy, as potential user and source of capital, was deeply identified with the horse and the carriage on which its family crest was emblazoned. But under Edward the upper class took to the car, just as it had briefly taken to the bicycle a decade earlier. In the census of 1901 the trade 'motormaker' was first mentioned; but dictionaries still maintained that 'automobile' was an adjective and 'garage' not an English word. By 1910 it was becoming widely recognized that the advent of the car was changing fundamentally not only the roads of England, but the cities and villages as well.

Today, as one stands at a week-end in summer at one of London's major exits on to the Brighton road, breathing exhaust fumes and listening to the gears as the lights change, one's mind goes back wistfully to the scene described by Charlie Chaplin at the beginning of the century.

> On Sunday morning, along the Kennington Road one could see a smart pony and trap outside a house, ready to take a vaudevillean for a ten-mile drive as far as Norwood or Merton, stopping on the way back at the various pubs, the White Horse, the Horns and the Tankard in the Kennington Road. As a boy of 12 I often stood outside the Tankard watching these illustrious gentlemen alight from their equestrian outfits to enter the lounge bar, where the élite of vaudeville met, as was their custom on a Sunday to take a final 'one' before going home to the midday meal. How glamorous they were, dressed in chequered suits and grey bowlers, flashing their diamond rings and tie-pins!

The change from the horse-drawn to the mechanically propelled vehicle did not take place without a period of transition; this was dominated by the bicycle and tricycle, using first solid rubber tyres and later the inflated tyres devised by John Boyd Dunlop, a Belfast veterinary surgeon. The invention of the pneumatic tyre made the bicycle an acceptable means of transport for ladies. As Gwen Raverat puts it:

> And soon after that everyone had bicycles, ladies and all; and ladies bicycling became the smart thing in Society, and the lords and ladies had their pictures in the papers, riding along in the park, in straw boater hats. We were then promoted to wearing baggy knickerbockers under our frocks, and over our white frilly drawers. We thought this horridly improper, but rather grand. . . .

Ladies invited out to dinner, she relates, would tuck up their trains and take intrepidly to their bicycles. In London, whilst

An outing at Yarmouth, 1906

the conservatives of fashion continued to ride horseback in Rotten Row, the more radical élite put their bicycles on top of a growler and resorted to Battersea Park, where male breeches anxiously awaited the appearance of female knickerbockers. The bicycle liberated the ladies both from the voluminous skirt and from the chaperone.

In the vanguard of the movement that popularized the bicycle, so causing society to abandon it, was that forward-looking man, H. G. Wells, who also had a keen eye for the shapely calf beneath the knickerbocker. The hero and heroine of his novel *Wheels of Chance* are identified with the bicycle in the same way that the later heroes and heroines of Dornford Yates are identified with the Rolls-Royce. Wells wrote his novel in a semi-detached house in Woking overlooking the railway.

I learned to ride my bicycle upon sandy tracks with none but God to help me. . . . I rode wherever Mr Hoopdriver rode in that story. . . . The bicycle in those days was still very primitive. The diamond frame had appeared but there was no free-wheel. You could only stop and jump off when the treadle was at its lowest point, and the brake was an uncertain plunger upon the front wheel. Consequently you were often carried on beyond your intentions, as when Mr Polly upset the zinc dust-bins outside the shop of Mr Rusper.

71

Toad is in the grip of his motoring mania

Nevertheless, the bicycle was the swiftest thing upon the roads in those days, there were as yet no automobiles and the cyclist had a lordliness, a sense of masterful adventure, that has gone from him altogether now.

By the time Mr Hoopdriver's many emulators took to the road, the smart set had their eye on the horseless carriage. Some may have had their vision of the future in much the same way as Mr Toad's old grey horse, which backed his canary-yellow caravan into the ditch, terrified by a 'small cloud of dust, advancing on them at incredible speed, while from the dust a faint "Poop-poop" wailed like an uneasy animal in pain'. Whatever the horse may have thought, Toad was in raptures. 'O what a flowery track lies spread before me henceforth! What dust-clouds shall spring up behind me as I speed on my reckless Way!' But before the way was open to reckless road toads and road hogs the Red Flag Act had to be repealed. This was achieved in 1896, when distinction was at last made between a traction engine and lighter vehicles, and the Local Government Board set the speed limit for the latter group of 12 m.p.h. In 1899 the first death due to a petrol-driven vehicle was recorded in England; 60 years later the total had reached a quarter of a million.

Largely because of the Red Flag Act the French and German motor industries had the advantage over ours; the first cars owned by Edward VII were a Mercedes and a Renault. The earliest British petrol-driven cars, such as the Arrol-Johnston, were copied from imported Panhards and Daimlers. The Arnold, the first British car to be produced in series, was

72

modelled on the Benz. The problems of the industry were aggravated by uncertainty whether the wave of the future might not favour cars driven by electricity or steam. Although no way to recharge a battery whilst running had yet been found, the relatively silent electric vehicle had its supporters. Other pioneers, like Mrs Raverat's Uncle William, chose a steam car. Uncle William's was a

> White Steam Car, which he named Betsey. . . . The Car was always breaking down and having to be given drinks of water with a teacup out of the nearest ditch. Sometimes it blew up and spattered us with orange spray out of the boiler; and at any steep hill it was no better than Aunt Sara's horses; it stopped and we all had to get out and push behind. . . .

In the earliest days of motoring it was an honourable practice that no moving motorist should pass by on the other side, leaving stranded a less fortunate fellow motorist. The fraternity of the road had acquired a new meaning since the days of highwaymen.

The designer and engineer who has the best claim to have made commercially the first all-British car is Dr Frederick Lanchester, a remarkable man, whose wide interests included, besides aerodynamics, Wagner's operas and Chinese jade. The second car that he produced contained numerous innovations, summed up as follows by Laurence Pomeroy: 'a horizontally opposed engine with two contra-rotating crankshafts . . . a live rear axle embodying a worm drive; electric ignition, and an epicyclic gearbox.' The specification is modern enough, but to outward appearance these early cars still took after their fathers, the coach or dog-cart. This was not surprising, since the chassis were made by coach-builders and were intended to tempt the wealthy man who

A steam car of 1902

A Lanchester touring car. The engine was alongside the driver's feet

associated speed and elegance with the horse-drawn carriage. The driver sat high on a box with a tiller under his right arm; he kept to the left of the road, but he sat on the right, because that was the side on which the coachman usually sat. His chauffeur, if he had one, inherited his name from those who had stoked traction engines. The chassis was fitted with a pair of large carriage lamps, which burned gas or acetylene; it was not until 1911 that the problem of recharging batteries was solved and the electrical circuit was completed.

The wheels of the early car looked as though a wheelwright had made them; often enough he had. The light-weight cycle-car, however, had wheels taking after its parent the tricycle. At the speeds at which horses drew vehicles solid rubber types had proved adequate; but bad roads and imperfect springing soon made it imperative to adapt J. B. Dunlop's invention for the motor car. This was successfully done by two descendants of a Huguenot family, William Harvey du Cros and his son Arthur. By the date at which Arthur du Cros was advancing money to the Countess of Warwick, and so becoming involved in the strange saga of the abortive sale of her correspondence with the late King Edward VII, du Cros was Managing Director of the Dunlop Rubber Company and worth £3 million. Early tyres were not robust; on one occasion a suffragette punctured a police car with a safety-pin. The plague of the puncture was alleviated before long, when the detachable wheel, perfected by Rudge Whitworth, finally replaced the original carriage wheel. Around the same time pressed-steel chassis frames were coming into production and car bodies

The 'motor-hansom', 1903

grew longer and lower. Resemblance to the coach persisted only in the heavy, closed car. The assumption that most of these would be chauffeur-driven was expressed in the lack of any protection for the front seat. Vauxhall made a car which had exactly the appearance of a horseless hansom cab. Until comparatively recently London taxicabs retained the look of the closed car of the Edwardian period.

The motor car, as an all-purpose vehicle, is usually regarded as having come of age in April 1900, when 65 cars of widely ranging make and design lined up near Hyde Park Corner for the start of a gruelling 1,000-mile test, intended to provide both manufacturers and the public with some basic evidence. Designers were still divided on the relative merits of steam or petrol; horizontal or vertical engines; two cylinders or four; belt transmission or chain and sprocket drive; air or water cooling and other problems which the trial was meant to solve. Equally important in the eyes of the sponsor, the Automobile Club of Great Britain and Ireland (later by courtesy of King Edward, the RAC), was the need to popularize motoring and convince the general public that it represented a reliable means of progression. One-day exhibitions were scheduled at the main centres of population, the proceeds to be donated to the Transvaal War Fund.

There was indeed much popular ignorance and, as usual, with ignorance went derision. One participant in the trial was so much exasperated by the attentions of small boys, who threw their caps in the path of his oncoming car, that he swore he would chastise the next to do so. When the moment came, he applied his brakes with such violence that he was thrown over his steering wheel on to the road. At least one small boy, however, was sufficiently impressed to take a day off from Harrow. He was J. T. C. Moore-Brabazon (Lord Brabazon of Tara) who was

A Gladiator in the Irish A.C. Reliability Trials, 1908

later to become an addict of both motor-racing and flying; the penalty of his truancy was to copy 1,000 lines of Greek verse. There were other casualties on the trial. One car turned a couple of somersaults on greasy tramlines in Bristol and a two-cylinder Daimler entered Newcastle with the co-driver standing on the step and controlling the direction of the front wheels with one foot. But on the whole the faith of the organizers was abundantly vindicated.

To stimulate the design of touring cars the RAC in 1905 started the Tourist Trophy event in the Isle of Man. In the first year it was won by a young Scot, John S. Napier, in an 18-h.p. Arrol-Johnston at an average of 33·9 m.p.h. In the following year the winner was a Welshman, the Hon. C. S. Rolls, son of Lord Llangattock, who was dealing in cars at Conduit Street and Earls Court. Only two years earlier he had begun his renowned partnership with Henry Royce, originally a manu-facturer of cranes in Manchester. The first Royce cars were twin-cylinder 10-h.p. light-weights, produced at a time when Montague Napier in Lambeth was making the six-cylinder cars which for elegance and reliability matched anything France or Germany could offer. But in 1908 Napier could produce nothing to beat the Rolls-Royce six-cylinder 'Silver Ghost', which from the first laid claim to silent running as one of its attributes. The more streamlined model of 1911 sold for £1,154 15s.

By this date many improvements had made life easier for the motorist. F. R. Simms, one of the founder-members of the RAC, had shown himself ahead of his time by fitting rubber

George Edwardes in a six-cylinder Rolls-Royce, 1908

An accident at Brooklands in 1907 involving Moore-Brabazon's Minerva

safety bumpers on the front of his car. Percy Riley had designed a three-speed gearbox of constant-mesh type. Windscreens, usually made to open in the middle because there were no wipers, were becoming a standard fitting, as were four-wheel brakes. H. F. S. Morgan introduced individual front-wheel suspension into the design of his three-wheelers. Many experiments were made with light one-cylinder cars and cyclecars as motoring became more popular. Morgan's Runabout, at first a single-seater, sold in 1910 for no more than £65. He was the son of Prebendary H. G. Morgan, Vicar of Stoke Lacy in Worcestershire, who helped to finance his venture. The son lived near Malvern after his marriage and some of the pioneer work was done in the workshops of the Public School.

Bookmakers at Brooklands

Road racing, then as now, was banned in England, and apart from hill-climbing tests at such places as South Harting and Shelsley Walsh, trying out new designs under conditions of stress

55 'The Dust Fiend'

presented a problem. It was overcome through the benefaction of Mr Locke-King, on whose Weybridge estate Brooklands was constructed. Shortly before the track was formally opened in 1907, S. F. Edge, driving single-handed in a Napier, averaged 65·9 m.p.h. over 24 hours. The first meetings at Brooklands were organized much like race-meetings; there were bookmakers and a paddock, where cars paraded, and drivers wore distinctively coloured caps and coats. In 1908 three cars, a Brasier, a Fiat and a Napier, lapped at over 100 m.p.h. It was at Brooklands in 1912 that Percy Lambert in a Talbot became the first to drive over 100 miles in one hour.

The fur-lined motoring coat

Relegation of high-speed testing to the track did nothing, of course, to abate the nuisance of the ordinary road hog, whose misdemeanours were aggravated by roads many of which degenerated into dust in summer and mud in winter. Local authorities, finding that spraying from water-carts did little to lay the dust and that spreading loose stones and gravel caused punctures and more serious accidents, began to experiment with tar and bitumen surfaces. There was at first a requirement that an oncoming motorist should stop if the driver of a horse-drawn vehicle raised his hand; but motorists were no doubt discouraged from passing too slowly by tales of members of their fraternity being slashed with whips by outraged carriage folk.

A motor bonnet

In 1907 *The Times* suggested hopefully that motorists might be obliged to reduce speed if use of the horn were prohibited. To enforce the speed limit, which in 1903 had risen to 20 m.p.h., local police forces were active in setting speed traps. The equestrian and pedestrian public was not reassured by the complaint of an Irish peer in the House of Lords that it was impossible for a car descending a steep hill to observe the limit. The need to identify offenders, as well as to raise revenue from the motorist, led in 1903 to legislation which required him to register his vehicle for a fee of £1, display a number plate and take out a licence at a charge of two guineas. A fee of 5s. was also imposed for a licence to drive; it did not occur to the authorities then, or for many years to come, to demand any proof that the driver was, in fact, capable of controlling a vehicle. In the first year 23,000 cars were registered, 8,500 of them in London; within six years the total had risen to 100,000.

The car like the bicycle influenced the clothing of the day. The early cars lacked both hood and windscreen, so the motorist needed protection against dust in summer, rain in winter and wind at all seasons. The formidable goggles worn by motoring pioneers added to the fear which they inspired in somnolent villages. The leisured Englishman, except for the yachtsman, has never taken to a flat peaked cap or *casquette*; motorists, apart from racing drivers, left this headgear to their chauffeurs and tried out instead various styles of cloth cap, worn in winter with ear-flaps. The chauffeur was heir to the former coachman's breeches and gaiters. Long dustcoats were necessary in summer and in wet weather tent-like capes, off which water would run. One enterprising designer, presumably Scottish, produced an indiarubber kilt. As overcoats of normal cut and cloth tended to inflate, motorists preferred heavy materials, such as leather and fur. The Englishman showed his lack of ostentation, as compared with the continental motorist, by wearing the fur on the inside.

Women took to motoring as keenly as men and innumerable styles of bonnet were designed for them. As motoring became more and more a part of ordinary life, the overlarge hats of the early period began to give way, except at garden-parties and other social functions, to cottage bonnets, toques and tweed hats of a more sporting kind, decorated perhaps with feathers. Veils were, of course, essential; as one advertisement put it, only a woman wearing a veil could expect to return fresh and smart from a drive, 'instead of showing dishevelled hair, a red nose adorned with smuts, discoloured cheeks and watery eyes'.

There can never have been a period in history when city streets displayed so wide a variety of means of conveyance. The open-topped horse-drawn omnibus was struggling for survival against the motor bus, the hansom against the taxicab and the electric trams against both. Beneath the city of London underground railways were burrowing. Steamboats carried passengers on the Thames; commuters from Blackheath and Greenwich found water transport particularly convenient. London and its rapidly expanding suburbs seemed in perpetual motion. By 1905 tramlines ran out to Richmond and Wimbledon. The trams, following a predestined course and discharging their passengers into the middle of the street, aggravated the congestion. The problem arose in London from the fact that the city had grown through the linking of clusters of villages on the outskirts; these retained their central density whilst through traffic demanded passage. In 1903 the far-sighted Medical

Road-menders in the middle of Piccadilly Circus in 1910. Notice the diversity of traffic—horse buses, a motor bus and taxicab, motor-cars and carriages

Officer of Health for Chelsea called for 'new main thorough-fares, wide enough to provide a clear way for six or eight lines of vehicles going at different speeds'. The thrift and myopia of ratepayers prevailed over these enlightened views.

London was not alone in its commuter problems, nor was Lancashire behindhand in devising solutions. Before the end of the nineteenth century Liverpool had tunnelled under the Mersey, so opening up the Cheshire side of the river for suburbanites. Dirt and foul air forced the Mersey Railway to abandon steam in 1903 and become the first railway in England to convert to electricity. Liverpool also pioneered in England the elevated railway, running into the heart of the city, such as had become familiar to visitors to New York. The Liverpool Overhead Railway was not only electrified, but boasted an escalator at Seaforth and automatic electric signalling equipment.

Electrification of suburban lines was forced upon railway companies by the competition of electric tramways. The Lancashire and Yorkshire Railway electrified the section from

Liverpool to Southport as early as 1904 and in the same year the North Eastern Railway electrified suburban services on Tyneside. Electrified mileage on tramways in towns doubled between 1900 and 1907; the tram was particularly welcome in hilly northern towns with cobbled streets, where horse-drawn public transport had long posed problems. Often the Corporation stepped in, as with the Blackburn trams (1899) and the Todmorden motor buses (1907). Other assets of the trams were that they did not add to the fumes of city streets and they had great carrying capacity; the London County Council's standard E/I model, which was introduced in 1907 and survived for 40 years, accommodated 78 passengers.

The horse bus, which was the victim of the tram and the motor bus, was a long time dying. Whilst experiments were being made with single-deck, wagonette bodies, running on steel tyres and powered by electric batteries, steam or petrol, the number of horse-drawn buses licensed in London actually increased in order to cope with the demand for transport. A peak of 3,736 licences was reached in 1901 and four years later the figure had only fallen to 3,484. By that date, however, a standard type of double-decker motor bus with solid rubber tyres had been evolved and continued in use with very little change for the next 15 years. Like its predecessor, it had an upper deck open to wind and weather, so that on wet days a forest of umbrellas rose above it. By 1908, 1,000 of these vehicles were plying in London; yet it was still possible for the chief officer of the LCC's tramways to prophesy that '20 years hence motor buses will be exhibited as curios in museums'. Had he said 'horse buses', he would have been right. The last in regular service was withdrawn on the evening of 4 August, 1914 on account of the requisitioning of horses for the war. The hansom was also in full retreat; 6,300 taxicabs were licensed in London in 1910.

As London traffic slowed, regular travellers went below ground in increasing numbers. Before the end of the nineteenth century the need had already arisen to provide cheap, fast transport for those who travelled daily to London, but preferred to live in the suburbs. Suburban steam railways existed

A motor bus

in the later Victorian era and one, the London, Chatham and Dover Railway, had brought its service into the centre of the City by means of a viaduct crossing the Thames at Blackfriars. But instead of adopting the Elevated Railway, London preferred to build tunnels. In Victoria's time plans were laid, legislation was enacted and engineers solved the problems of tunnelling and ventilation; only two items were needed—capital and some means of locomotion other than steam. Experiments were made with cable traction, but it was electricity that provided the solution. In November 1890 the Prince of Wales opened the first electric tube railway in the world—the City and South London Railway; it carried passengers from King William Street to Stockwell through a tunnel 10 feet 2 inches in diameter.

After that the remaining problems were financial. It may seem strange that in a thriving age of capital investment it proved impossible in the last decade of the nineteenth century to finance the development that alone could meet London's needs. The fact is, however, that the financiers judged the risk correctly; the cost of constructing and equipping tube railways proved so high that it has never been possible to ensure an adequate return on the investment. Since the opening of the Hampstead Tube in 1907, no further tube railways were opened, until the new Victoria Line became operational in 1969. That the Edwardian period saw the burgeoning of London's underground system was due to American capital. In the nineteenth century British capital had made a massive contribution to the development of the US; in the twentieth century the return flow began.

Excavating the Great Northern and City Tube, 1901

The harbinger was Charles Tyson Yerkes of Chicago. Yerkes was a man of vision. R. D. Blumenfeld mentions him in his diary for the year 1900:

> . . . he predicted to me that a generation hence London will be completely transformed; that some people will think nothing of living 20 or more miles from town owing to electrified trains. He also thinks that the horse and omnibus is doomed. Although he is a very shrewd man, I think he is a good deal of a dreamer.

James McNeill Whistler was another American dreamer; but some of his dreams were nightmares which came true. Blumenfeld wrote of him: 'His latest grievance is that Yerkes proposes to put up a gigantic power house in Chelsea for the electrification of the Underground, and as it is to have enormous chimneys towering into the sky, it will completely ruin the bend of

84

the Thames made famous by Turner.' Much was ruined in Edward's reign in the name of progress and economic development; plans were made for the ruination of a great deal more.

American help was not confined to the provision of capital. James Russell Chapman, who was Chief Engineer for Yerkes's Underground group, was an American. Lifts were supplied by the Otis Elevator Company and the Westinghouse system of signalling was introduced to control track circuits. The American word 'car' came into use instead of the British word 'carriage' and many were made by the American Car and Foundry Company. The American invasion was not to the liking of more traditionally minded British railwaymen, some of whom would not have been sorry to see these enterprises fail. When the Bakerloo was opened in 1906, it carried some 37,000 passengers on the first day; but for a time thereafter traffic fell off and in July the magazine *Railway Engineer* observed smugly, 'this tube railway may now be regarded as a beautiful failure'. The original plan had been to charge a 2*d.* fare to all destinations; but after a few months fares assessed according to distance were introduced. Season tickets became available towards the end of 1906. An attempt was made to estimate how much time and money was saved by those crossing London from Piccadilly Circus to Baker Street by

Waiting for the lifts at the Bank Station, 1901

Tube. The Bakerloo took seven minutes and cost 2*d*.; the omnibus at the same price took 20 minutes; the horse cab completed the journey in 15 minutes for a fare of 1*s*. 6*d*.

Two of the most familiar features of the modern underground system had not been commonly adopted in Edwardian times. Although the moving staircase had been invented, it was not generally brought into use until later; the public at large still seemed willing to use their legs. An escalator was installed at Earls Court in October 1911; but it aroused some mistrust and a man with a wooden leg was hired to show passengers that even he could ascend and descend without danger. Another essential facility of the modern system is the junction between divergent lines. Here, too, development was slow; apart from the junction at Camden Town on the Hampstead Line, no others came into regular use in the years before the First World War. The Bakerloo, however, provided facilities at Paddington in December 1913 for its passengers to transfer to the Great Western Railway and two escalators were installed there.

The Underground made changes in the lives of Londoners; it enabled them to leave the City on short excursions or to quit it altogether and become commuters. It was a major factor in producing the urban sprawl that is one of the least attractive aspects of the 600 or so square miles ruled today by the Greater London Council. It has proved an efficient system; those who think it would have operated more conveniently if designed as one whole would do well to recall that its different parts came into existence at different times, conjured into life by groups of enterprising capitalists of more than one nationality.

It should not be forgotten, in contemplation of so many innovations, that the steam train was still the principal means of transport; indeed one historian of the railways has called the period up to 1914 'the Railways' golden era'. A very extensive, if imperfectly co-ordinated, network of independent railways covered the country already; only some 1,200 miles were added in England and Wales between 1900 and 1913. The last major railway company, the Great Central, had made its appearance at Marylebone in 1899. Most of the great nineteenth-century struggles for profitable routes and traffic had resulted in adjustment or amalgamation, though the rivalry of the Great Western Railway and the London and South Western Railway for the boat-train passengers from Southampton and Plymouth led to high speeds, as well as a major disaster at the approaches to Salisbury Station on 1 July 1906. Three years earlier an express of the GWR had averaged 67 m.p.h. over the 194 miles between Exeter and Paddington. High speeds were also registered over shorter mileages; runs from Darlington to York and Leicester to Nottingham were regularly made in even time.

Travel by train was cheap at a third-class rate of 1d. per mile: a return fare from London to Newcastle cost only £2 5s. 3d. It was also relatively safe, though most companies were slow to substitute electric for gas lighting, despite the risk of fire after an accident; engineers were familiar with the dynamo, but were reluctant to add to the weight to be hauled. In general, standards of comfort and convenience were rising; steam heating was replacing the old-fashioned cylindrical foot-warmer. Pullman sleepers for first-class passengers had been introduced on long-distance trains well before the end of the nineteenth century, as well as a corridor leading to a lavatory; but trains fully connected by corridors were not in general use for all classes until nearly a decade later. Corridors reduced the apprehensions of lonely female travellers at wayside halts, as they cowered in their 'Ladies Only' compartments; but in the first class it continued to be *de rigueur* for a lady to be accompanied by her maid and to be met on arrival at her destination. The London and North Western Railway provided a travelling typist for its businessman's special, linking Broad Street and Birmingham via Euston.

With the corridor came the restaurant car, offering lunch for 2s. 6d.; it replaced the packed picnic baskets, which courteous railway companies had previously provided at passengers' request. Food at station buffets, however, was already coming in for criticism; an article on the subject in *Punch* was entitled 'None but the Brave can stand the Fare'. Queen Victoria had always refused to eat a meal in a moving train; her son had no such inhibitions. The London and North Western and

87

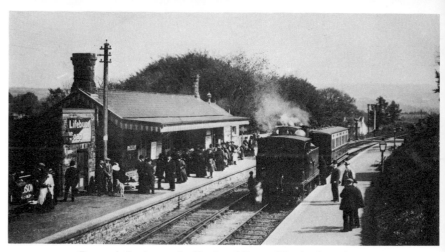

Devynock Station on the Neath and Brecon Line in the early 1900s

Caledonian Railways built for him a magnificent dining-saloon, which won a Grand Prix in Paris. The dining compartment was 20 feet long and panelled in walnut and mahogany. The kitchen contained complete gas-cooking equipment and there were no less than three refrigerators, including one for the wine.

Whilst expresses live on in the record books and memories of railway enthusiasts, literature has found a place for some of the wayside halts of obscure branch lines. Here is one recalled with affection by Rudyard Kipling:

The train stopped in a blaze of sunshine at Framlyngham Admiral, which is made up entirely of the nameboard, two platforms, and an overhead bridge, without even the usual siding. . . . One could hear the drone of conversation along the carriages and, scarcely less loud, the drone of the bumble-bees in the wallflowers up the bank.

There was still time to stop and listen in Edwardian England, even if almost everyone was on the move.

As in the previous century, railwaymen were largely recruited from surplus agricultural workers and they carried with them into the industry much of the friendliness of the farm. The Devonshire diarist and naturalist Bruce Frederick Cummings (Barbellion) recorded an excursion in August 1911.

Caught the afternoon train to C——, but unfortunately forgot to take with me either watch or tubes (for insects). So I applied to the station-master, a youth of about 18, who is also signalman, porter, ticket-collector, and indeed very factotal—even to the extent of providing me with empty match-boxes. I agreed with him to be called by three halloos from the viaduct just before the evening train came in.

The relation of railway employees with the public was happier than with the railway companies, whose attitude tended to be one of autocracy tempered by paternalism. The largest unskilled union, the Amalgamated Society of Railway Servants, called a strike in 1900 against the Taff Vale Company, which won substantial damages against the Society, after an appeal to the House of Lords. In 1911 a general strike was declared on the railways. Tempers rose and Winston Churchill, who was Home Secretary, called out the troops. Under Asquith's influence, however, conciliation prevailed; he called together representatives of the unions and the companies, most of whom on this occasion met for the first time across a negotiating table. Two years later the major unions, except the Associated Society of Locomotive Engineers and Firemen (ASLEF), combined to form the giant National Union of Railwaymen. ASLEF, the oldest of the railway unions, remained

Balloons at Hurlingham Park Sports Ground, 1908

The first flight of a power-driven, man-carrying aeroplane at Kitty Hawk, 1903. Orville Wright is piloting the aeroplane and his brother, Wilbur, is on foot

as a monument to the differentiated status of the skilled worker.

The Edwardian era, which made such important advances in transport along the ground and under it, saw also man's first successful application of power to rise and travel above it. He had long been familiar with the balloon, both in theory and practice, and towards the end of Victoria's reign experiments had been made with gliders; but the aspiring aviator was still at the mercy of the wind. By providing the balloon with propeller and engine he acquired a measure of control; but the airship thus constructed was far from satisfactory. In 1903 Stanley Smith flew an airship from the Crystal Palace over St Paul's, but he was unable to return, as he had intended, to his take-off point. In spite of the progress made in Germany by Count Zeppelin, the future lay with machines that were heavier than air.

The great leap forward was made by the Wright brothers at Kitty Hawk, North Carolina; when their powered machine rose from the ground, the age of aeronautics began. Wilbur Wright came over to France in 1908 and his feats impressed observers. Major B. F. S. Baden-Powell commented, 'That Wilbur Wright is in possession of a power which controls the fate of nations is beyond dispute.' In 1909 a Frenchman, Louis Blériot, made the first Channel-crossing, flying from Baraques, near Calais. A few days earlier Hubert Latham, starting from Sandgate, had failed to reach the French coast and was rescued from the sea by a French destroyer. Both these flights were made in monoplanes, but experiments with biplanes and even triplanes were being made. In 1910 C. S. Rolls lost his life in a Wright biplane. The first all-British machine to fly was a

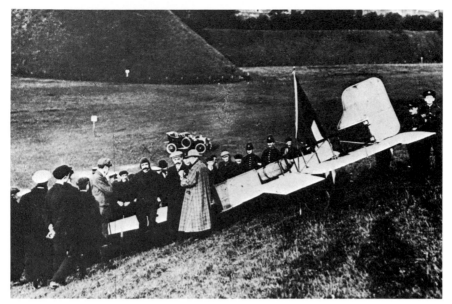

Blériot after his flight over the Channel in 1909

nine-h.p. triplane constructed by A. V. Roe. The first pilot's
licence was issued to Lord Brabazon, who later commemorated
the distinction in the registration number of his car—FLY 1.

At a time of international tension in Europe it was not to be
expected that military men and patriots would ignore the
possibilities of the new discovery. In the House of Commons

Brabazon about to set off on the flight which earned him his Pilot's Certificate No. 1

Arthur du Cros, who had already contributed £6,000 towards the cost of the first airship constructed in Britain, was responsible for the inclusion of funds for aeronautics in the Navy and Army estimates for 1909. In the following year the Women's Aerial League was formed 'to stir up our country not to be left behind in this important branch of future warfare'. The first competition for military aircraft took place at Farnborough in August 1912. Two years later the Royal Flying Corps had the chance to win its spurs. The women of England, suffering under the raids of Zeppelins, later had their chance to do some serious thinking about the future of aerial warfare. A further 42 years of technology carried the human race from Kitty Hawk to Hiroshima.

Further Reading

H. Ellis, *British Railway History* (Volume II)
F. A. Talbot, *Motor Cars and Their Story*
L. T. C. Rolt, *Picture History of Motoring*
Underground and London Transport—see booklets issued by London Transport and British Railways Board

V

Health, Food and Holidays

Nobody planned the growth of England's cities in the nineteenth century; nobody clearly foresaw that at the end of it 77 per cent of the population would be urban dwellers. The result of this lack of foresight was that the Edwardian city was over-congested and insanitary and the mortality rate was high. This was especially true of the child population; in 1901 infant mortality per 1,000 births was 138. Jack London draws a pathetic picture of children dancing:

> There is one beautiful sight in the East End, and one only, and it is the children dancing in the street when the organ-grinder goes his round. It is fascinating to watch them, the new-born, the next generation, swaying and stepping . . . weaving rhythms never taught in dancing school. . . . But there is a Pied Piper of London who steals them all away.

As we have seen, the reaction of many people to the squalor of the cities was to move out, if they had the means to do so; but there were some who set themselves to improve the conditions. Industrialism, which had created most of the problems, had also supplied some of the means of solving them. The development of engineering enabled water to be brought in more readily and sewage to be removed. Purer and more plentiful water permitted higher standards of hygiene; legislators and administrators recognized—some with surprise—that human beings no more lived in filth because they liked it, than pigs lived in sties. In the latter part of the nineteenth century

93

Children dancing in the street to an organ, 1901

city streets were better paved and electricity was beginning to be used for street-lighting, as well as for illuminating the homes of the rich.

On the improved foundation provided by technology, medical science could build. Lister, whose long life spanned both the Victorian and Edwardian eras, had made surgery relatively safe by the discovery of antisepsis. Pasteur and Koch had evolved the new science of bacteriology and, as a result, doctors were forming a clearer idea of how disease was carried. In 1896 Dr Ronald Ross of the Indian Medical Service established the connection between malaria and the anopheline mosquito; it came too late to help the retired Anglo-Indians in Cheltenham, but it was a boon to their sons and nephews in Bombay and Calcutta. In the following year the Seamen's Hospital Society, concerned about the importation of diseases that were not endemic, set up in London the Hospital and School for Tropical Diseases. Before the end of the century a London electrical engineer had taken the first X-ray photographs for clinical purposes. The Curies discovered radium and in 1902 the Free Cancer Hospital opened a new department for the practice of electrotherapy.

There was still much ignorance; even men in high position believed that appendicitis might be contagious. Insulin for the treatment of diabetics was unknown. None knew that rickets,

94

which was so prevalent, was caused by deficiencies of diet. But much of the fatalist attitude of the nineteenth century towards illness and early death was disappearing. The medical profession and the philanthropists who gave their help were increasingly confident that scientific research would alleviate, or even, in time, eradicate many of the scourges of humanity. Apart from cancer, tuberculosis chiefly held the attention of humane Edwardians. In 1901 a TB Congress was held in London and a Royal Commission was set up to inquire into means of stamping out the disease. In 1905 the micro-organism causing syphilis was detected and shortly after the Wasserman test was introduced. The area opened up to medical science by these and other discoveries was so vast that the profession became increasingly specialized. For the general practitioner it was more difficult to keep up with the latest developments; for the specialist it was harder to remember that the human mind and body require to be treated as one entity.

Some of the new knowledge, which had as yet scarcely reached the arena of public discussion, tended to undermine Victorian confidence that man, whilst maintaining a deferential attitude towards his Maker, could largely solve his problems by reliance on his own reason and will power. Freud's excursions into the subconscious had revealed an underworld where man was powerless against the forces of unreason, driven blindly by sexual urges which he resisted at his peril. Even those who might be prepared to dismiss Freud's hypotheses as biased and unscientific could not ignore the implications for human behaviour of the working of the ductless glands. Sir W. M. Bayliss published his *Psychopathology of Everyday Life* in 1904. In 1905 E. H. Starling described the action of hormones, and adrenaline action was analyzed by Sir Henry Dale in 1906. Before the specialists of the new science of endocrinology, man stood exposed as a creature whose responsibility for his own actions rested on a delicate balance of inner forces, of whose working the victim was ignorant.

It should not be assumed that the advance made by the medical profession had freed it from prejudice. There remained a resolute refusal to regard hypnosis as a legitimate form of anaesthesia, let alone a means of treating mental aberration. Bonesetters and chiropractors, who had not acquired the traditional medical qualification, were regarded as outlaws; the fact that they could make men whole was no extenuation. Sir Herbert Barker, whose treatments had relieved the suffering of such men as Bernard Shaw and Rudyard Kipling, was execrated by the British Medical Association and in 1911 an anaesthetist who had worked for him was struck off the medical register. Doctors had progressed in their ability to treat venereal disease, but they were loath to consider such problems as contraception and sexual maladjustment as coming within their purview. Their preference for drawing a veil over these aspects of life and society were, of course, shared by the general public. The *Daily Chronicle*, reviewing Havelock Ellis's volume *Sexual Inversion*, observed: 'We cannot take the view that the book has any scientific value whatever. . . .' Fortunately, Ellis persisted and the six volumes of his *Studies in the Psychology of Sex* appeared at intervals between 1897 and 1910. He was very much in the vanguard of thought with his interest in all the new sciences of psychology, psychopathology, eugenics and social anthropology.

Although the Edwardian era was seminal, in terms of these new branches of knowledge, the revolution in the thinking of ordinary men, which has followed, has been of more recent date. There was one earlier revolution of thought, however, which had begun to show results before the First World War. Whatever one may think of the validity of the Utilitarian creed, as a philosophy of life, there is no doubt about the profound and beneficial effect exercised by its insistence that human happiness is a norm to be achieved by reason and common sense. It followed from this creed that obedience to an inscrutable providence did not require that the majority of the people should exist in misery, content with the thought that, if they nevertheless remained virtuous, they would reap their reward in a better world to come. The followers of Jeremy Bentham set about to create conditions in which children could survive to manhood and men could face old age without fear. This doctrine combined well with theories of preventive medicine that were increasingly coming into practice. Notification of certain diseases was made compulsory; and an Act of 1898 required parents to have their infants inoculated against smallpox within six months of birth, unless they substantiated their objections before a Court. Ten years later Sir Almroth

An operation in Charing Cross Hospital in 1901

Wright, the pathologist at St Mary's Hospital, set up a department of therapeutic inoculation, where he developed an anti-typhoid serum.

Philanthropy, if it is to be effective, must usually be backed by proof that investment in human welfare will show a

Waiting to buy trimmings of meat at the market

return. Enlightened industrialists had begun to recognize that accidents were inefficient and that a healthy labour force was more productive. The fact that employers were using more skilled labour helped them to draw the right conclusions. For those who were slow to do so, the State was increasingly prepared to step in by controlling hours of work, as in the mines, or setting up Trade Boards to fix minimum wages in industries that had not regulated themselves. At the end of the nineteenth century the first women factory inspectors had been appointed. The first attempt to deal with the health of the working population on a national scale was the National Insurance Act of 1911, which also included provision against unemployment in industries in which it was most prevalent. Until that date, only the Friendly Societies, which continued to play an important role under the Act, had stood between a worker who lost his health and the grim prospect of the workhouse.

The evils of malnutrition had impressed themselves upon the authorities at the time of the Boer War, when it had been found necessary to reject a disturbingly high percentage of the recruits who presented themselves. This was a serious threat to the security of a nation that depended upon volunteers for its defence. At the turn of the century a cumulative impact was being made by the publication of the final volumes of Charles Booth's great survey, *Life and Labour in London*, which painted an alarming picture of misery and want in the capital of the world's richest Empire. Booth found that over 30 per cent of the population of London was living at a level below that necessary to maintain 'mere physical efficiency'. His findings were corroborated by the publication in 1901 of Seebohm Rowntree's researches, entitled *Poverty, A Study of Town Life*, in which he concluded that 28 per cent of the inhabitants of York could not afford a diet adequate to sustain a normal day's work. From this point the analysis of nutrition and metabolism in terms of vitamins and calories advanced rapidly.

Whilst lack of purchasing power was the root cause of the evil, the transplantation of country folk into urban surroundings seems also to have contributed to the inadequacy of their diet. It is true that agricultural wages were low and the picture of healthy peasants eating their wholesome food in their clean, comfortable cottages is largely imaginary; but there were at least seasons of the year when extra money could be made, when a pig was slaughtered, or there was a local glut of fruit or home-grown vegetables. At such times dietary deficiencies could in some degree be remedied in the country; but for the townsman all seasons passed alike with little or no opportunity to eat more appetizing and nourishing foods. In the lower bracket of earners about two-thirds of the weekly pay-packet had to be spent on food; household budgets rarely included fresh meat more than once a week and there was a monotonous diet of bread and margarine with cheese and sometimes kippers or bacon. After these modest purchases, little remained to pay rent, clothe a family and redeem the goods in pawn. Women went on the streets to get the mere necessities of life; children went to school so hungry that it was impossible for them to learn.

This desperate situation was alleviated in the last quarter of the nineteenth century not so much by the wisdom of statesmen or the appeals of charity as by the development of natural resources in distant continents, by improvements in the preservation of foodstuffs and by the introduction of bulk transportation. Grain from the prairies of North America sent prices tumbling in Britain; in the 1890s the cost of the 4-lb. loaf fell to 6*d*. and rose only slowly during the subsequent decade. Refrigerated meat from Australia, New Zealand and Argentina was within the price range of those to whom it had been a rare luxury. Fish caught in the North Sea and packed in ice reached the tables of people who hitherto had eaten only salt fish. Fish and chip shops in the cities did a thriving trade. Resourceful British farmers, cutting their losses on beef, mutton and grain, turned to milk production. In 1902 it was estimated that ordinary wage-earners were eating annually 10 lb. of cheese per head and 15 lb. of butter and drinking 8½ gallons of milk.

Poverty became more tolerable when one penny would buy a small loaf or two thick slices of bread and butter. For the same price two bloaters or two bananas could be got. Condensed milk and meat paste was obtainable in penny tins. In the old-fashioned coffee-shops, where working men sat in pews to eat their midday dinners, a portion of beef or mutton or steak and kidney pudding was to be had for 4*d*., to be followed by jam roll or rice pudding for 1*d*. There might be a special offer of 'baked side view' (half a sheep's head) for 3½*d*. For the night-worker or night wanderer there was the mobile coffee-stall, strategically placed near a bridge, crossroads or railway station, where for twopence the rigours of a cold night could be mitigated by a large cup of tea and a fried egg.

In many working-class homes in the cities wives got up early to pack up a midday meal for their husbands, who took it with them to work as their fathers had done on the farm. But a new class of urban worker had come into existence, whose status debarred him from carrying his lunch to the office where he worked. The rapidly multiplying race of clerks and office-workers demanded a new kind of catering and their ranks were being continuously expanded by young women, working as typists or telephonists, who did not wish to eat in a public house

The Aerated Bread Company's Depot at Ludgate Hill

or old-style coffee-shop. Tea-shops and cafés provided for this clientele a cheap, quick meal in more genteel surroundings; Joseph Lyons and the Aerated Bread Company met the demand. They were able to do so because the age of standardized food, hygienically packed and pleasing to the eye, had begun. The city workers no longer knew who had baked their bread or where the fish they ate had been caught. Their tea-dust, which then cost 1*s.* per pound retail, had not yet been put into bags; but already their vegetables were brought to table as they are today, swimming in the water in which they had been overboiled.

But when we think of food in connection with the Edwardian Age, our minds turn more often to César Ritz than to Joseph Lyons. The gourmet, above all others, has the right to look back on that age as a golden one. Seldom in human history can such rich food have been prepared so regularly by so many for so few; if the arts, in general, did not flourish, at least the culinary art reached new heights. The King, because his tastes and his paunch were pronounced and his cures well publicized, is often regarded as a gourmand, whose gross appetites prefigured those of his more opulent subjects. This judgment is less than fair to Edward, who was a discerning eater and, at least in his later years, a sparing one. It is true that the day began at Sandringham with haddock or bloater, eggs, bacon, chicken and woodcock, when in season, and that it often ended with a midnight snack featuring plover's eggs, ptarmigan and salmon; but the King was content on many evenings with tripe for supper. He was more discriminating than many of his fellow gourmets in his preference for lean, well-done meat and fruit instead of pudding.

The gargantuan repast was not, of course, an Edwardian innovation; in Victorian times even the bourgeoisie had thought nothing of sitting down to a family dinner of eight or ten courses. What strikes one today, however, is not so much the length of their menus as the inordinate number of courses of fish, meat and game, both hot and cold. Rosa Lewis of the Cavendish, who is credited with the discovery that young people, after the ball is over, prefer eggs and bacon and beer to more caviar and champagne, was noted for her balanced menus; but a

The Trocadero, Piccadilly

typical ten-course dinner might include, after the soup: Truite froide, Blanchailles, Soufflé de Cailles, Pièce de Bœuf à la gêlée, Jambon de Prague and Poularde, topped off by a savoury after the salad and sweet. When Auguste Oddenino chose a menu for the delectation of Lieutenant-Colonel Newnham-Davis, whose column 'Dinners and Diners' appeared in the *Pall Mall Gazette*, the first six courses were: Hors d'œuvres Russes, Pot-au-feu, Sole Waleska, Noisette d'Agneau Lavallière, Parfait de Foie-gras and Cailles en cocotte. One is not surprised to learn that Newnham-Davis followed the example of his sovereign by taking a cure every year at Marienbad or Carlsbad.

London abounded in great French and Italian *restaurateurs* and chefs. César Ritz presided at the hotel that still bears his name and was served by Escoffier, who once cooked frogs' legs in paprika and named them, with Gallic wit, 'nymphes à la rose'. Descending the social scale, one might arrive at Romano's in the Strand, where the ladies were often ladies of the stage and the gentlemen were gentlemen of the Turf or the Press. Romano's was strictly for a night out without the wife:

> *At Romano's—Italiano's*
> *It's a Paradise in the Strand*
> *At Romano's—as Papa knows—*
> *Where the wines and the women are grand!*

Good food was not exorbitant at the Trocadero. Edgar Wallace, having found a friend to stand him lunch, prices it as follows: 'The fish was filleted Sole Borghese, which knocked him for half-a-dollar; the bird was pheasant at 4*s*. 6*d*. I finished up with a Melba pear, 2*s*. and a glass of most glorious brandy, just a thimbleful of 2*s*. 6*d*. 1830 Cognac.' This was a special occasion; but Sir Lawrence Jones recalls how, when he was an impecunious barrister, 'We could dine for half-a-crown, or at a pinch for a florin, in Soho, and dine pretty well; even at the Union Club . . . I rarely paid more than 3*s*. or 4*s*. for a dinner and a good deal less for luncheon'.

All Edwardian menus bear witness to the increasing use of refrigeration. Salt and ice were freely employed in what were often referred to as 'freezing machines'. In the country a thatched ice stack, or an ice pit would be prepared during the winter. Colonel Meinertzhagen describes one in his *Diary of a Black Sheep*.

At Mottisfont we had a most useful little covered-in pit in which ice could be stored. It was situated in a clump of trees behind the stables, where it was completely shaded and consisted of a brick chamber excavated from the ground so that the top was level with the surface, which was slightly vaulted. . . . It was capable of holding about four tons of ice. After a heavy fall of snow all the gardeners and grooms would shovel snow in, trample it well down into ice and throughout the summer we always had as much ice as we wanted. We never had ice from any other source.

It was a good system, but it depended upon the supply of gardeners and grooms.

Ample domestic staff, both to cook and to serve, was indeed an essential feature of Edwardian meals, which

103

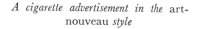

A cigarette advertisement in the art-nouveau style

would have scarcely admitted of any intervals unless one course had followed quickly upon another. The cookery books of the period show how seriously the Edwardian housewife was expected to take her duties. Recipes begin with warnings such as 'This dish takes two days to prepare'. An account of how to dress loin of mutton like roe venison includes the injunction, 'Leave it so eight days, but turn each piece every day'. Even more disconcerting to the modern cook are the two stern sentences with which *The Cookery Book of Lady Clark of Tillypronie* (1909) embarks on the subject of turtles. 'The turtle must be put in straw in the cellar and given water every two or three hours. It should be beheaded at night, and left hanging neck downwards.'

What the Edwardian male drank and smoked was as important to him as what he ate; both liquor and tobacco were major sources of revenue to the Exchequer. In 1909 duty on 1 lb. of tobacco went up to 8*d*. and tobacconists complained, 'The 5*d*. packet of cigarettes is doomed.' (It would have contained 25 Wild Woodbines.) Yet pipe-smokers could still get a ¼-lb. tin of Embassy Mixture for 2*s*. and those who wished to assert their social standing by smoking a cigar could buy seven

The bar in a West End public house

''Appy 'Ampstead.' Bank Holiday, *1902*

Rajahs for 1*s*. In London women were becoming addicted to cigarettes, though to smoke them in public was still frowned on.

In high society tastes in wine were changing; the King preferred, instead of the massive potations of claret of earlier periods, a light Chablis and extra-dry champagne, produced specially for the English market. Among his poorer subjects beer, with an original gravity of 1055°, was still a reasonably strong drink; but here, too, fashions were shifting. In 1900 the Bass Brewery in the Mile End Road produced only mild and stout; but as sugar came more within the purchasing range of working men, they mixed more bitter with their mild. Powerful stouts were diluted with beers to make porter, which sold for 3*d*. a quart. Those with a liking for 'a drop of the hard stuff' could buy a bottle of whisky for 3*s*. 6*d*.

The interest of legislators and industrialists in the health of the workers sustained the temperance propaganda, which had been such a feature of the Victorian era. Great numbers of tracts and leaflets continued to be distributed by such bodies as the Band of Hope and the Salvation Army. Non-conformist opinion backed their efforts, maintaining, both in Parliament and outside, that too many public houses were licensed and that they stayed open too long; normal hours were from 6 a.m.

to 11 p.m. It is a fact that in 1900 there were 30 per cent more public houses than there are today with our greater population: on the other hand, more clubs hold licences today than was the case 60 years ago. Women were, of course, particularly active in temperance work; membership of the British Women's Total Abstinence Union reached its peak (154,000) in Edward's reign. Most of their zeal was directed to the intemperance of the working man, which brought his wife and children to ruin; but women were not immune from periodic indulgence. Florence White recalls how, when she was working in Hoxton, she was surprised to come across two small girls commiserating with one another about the approach of Christmas; they were inured to the drunkenness of their fathers, but at Christmas their mothers got drunk as well.

Employers were slow to recognize that paid holidays might also contribute to the well-being, and thus the productivity, of their employees; but there was an increasing tendency to stretch the August Bank Holiday, and 'Wakes Weeks' in Lancashire were well established. Many domestic employers gave their servants a week or two off. For the less fortunate, there were cheap day excursions by train; a trip to Southend cost only 3s. and for double that fare a tripper could spend a day at Margate or Ramsgate. The trains were fast as well as cheap; in 1901 the 50 miles to Brighton from Victoria were covered in only 53½ minutes.

A concert party on the beach at Southend

The seaside holiday was essentially a family holiday and the pier shows, with clowns and nigger minstrels, and the donkey-rides on the beach, provided something for everybody. For the aged there was

Bathing costume 1902

the hooded wheel-chair, with two large wheels behind and one in front; it was licensed according to whether it was drawn by a person or pony (Class E), or by 'an ass or by a goat or goats' (Class G). Some seaside occupations were essentially male; as Gaby Deslys sang:

When I take my bain de mer
All the boys just come and stare.

By present-day standards they did not have a great deal to stare at. Bathing-costumes at the beginning of the century were not only made of materials such as serge and corduroy, but had bloomers to the knees and skirts to mid-thigh. At some resorts bathing-huts for men and for women were severely segregated. Before 1914, however, the liberation of women had extended to their bathing attire and designers, throwing caution to the winds, were going in for cotton, which clings when wet to the contours of the body.

The resorts catered for everybody. Fred Willis has recounted how at Yarmouth there was a holiday hotel run for men only by a formidable lady known as Ma Powell. Her guests, who got full board for a week for one guinea, were called Ma Powell's lambs. Their bachelor status was sufficiently well known in Yarmouth to attract to the neighbourhood soon after breakfast on a fine morning 'a delightful cross-section of the young and most enterprising members of the female population'.

Even mother claimed her holiday. The earlier tradition, by which she would shop for the family and then, husband permitting, leave the cooking to the landlady, was dying out in favour of either full board or bed and breakfast. The roving life of the 'b. and b.' clientele meant a great expansion of the catering trade. Boarding-houses in popular resorts like Eastbourne and Hove would provide couples sharing a room with full board for as little as 21s. a week; if there was a bathroom and running water available, instead of the standard marble-topped washstand with its jug and basin, the price might rise to 25*s*. or even 30*s*. at the height of the season. Hotels, of course, cost more and ranged all the way from a residential hotel or dignified boarding-house to a Grand Hotel with doorman and 'boots' in livery.

In many resorts a clash of interests had emerged between the summer visitors, especially the day-trippers, and the residents, who had fled from contact with the masses and had hoped that the estrangement would prove permanent. Retired couples with a pension and middle-class families with private means had had the idea of spending the winter, as well as the summer, where they could breathe the ozone and resinous exhalation of pine trees, instead of the fog and fumes of an industrial town. Whilst the inland watering-places—Bath, Tunbridge Wells, Matlock and the like—maintained themselves, it was the seaside towns that expanded most rapidly as all the year round habitats. All along the coastline villas and bungalows were springing up beside the hotels and boarding-houses provided for the transients. The resorts of the South and South-East grew with particular speed all the way from Margate to Torquay; Cornwall was still too remote and in 1901 only Newquay had achieved the status of a resort with a population of more than 3,000. Many of these resorts made special efforts to attract 'a good class' of resident, even if this meant discouraging trippers, and local enterprises catering to the mass. Where it was already too late for this policy to be applied, a more select suburb grew up for the middle class next to the resort that was losing its distinction: thus Hove was the neighbour of Brighton; Broadstairs of Margate; Westcliff of Southend; and Frinton of Clacton. Between 1901 and 1911 the population of Southend grew from 29,000 to 63,000.

As the railways had brought the great centres of population within comparatively easy reach of the sea, the select resorts tried to gratify their well-to-do residents by assuring them of a dull, drab Sunday, calculated to please the Sabbath-loving as much as it offended the week-end tripper. It was, after all, the former who paid the rates. Thus Bournemouth banned

Bournemouth orchestra with its conductor, Dan Godfrey, in the Winter Garden

Sunday trains until 1914, and 15 more years were to pass before excursion steamers were scheduled on Sundays. No bands played on Sundays in the gardens or on the esplanades; piers at these sabbatarian resorts were closed against those who might otherwise purchase the vulgar, if comic, postcards, which began to find favour at the seaside around 1905. A peep at 'What the Butler Saw' had to be reserved for a week-day. Eastbourne went so far as to forbid allotment-holders to dig them on Sunday. *Punch* summed up:

> Saturday and Monday, and every working day in a summer week, Bournemouth is blithe and gay. Steamers are running hither and thither, wagonettes, coaches, gardens with music, excellent bands on well-appointed pier, concerts, donkey-riding, *al fresco* refreshments, clowns, niggers—in fact, everything that is considered by the majority as constituting a 'appy 'oliday is to be found, at its best, at Bournemouth. But every Saturday night, long before the stroke of twelve, bands, lights, cocoa-nuts, niggers, donkey-boys, and all things and people that make quiet life impossible, vanish as if by magic, not to be heard of or seen again till Monday morning .... Sunday papers arrive late from town.... At Bournemouth on Sunday there is no four-horse coach, no horn blowing; I saw no motors, nor heard raucous cries of journal-vendors.

An exclusive policy, favouring the residents, certainly yielded results; rateable values in Bournemouth increased from £102,350 to nearly £791,000 in the period from 1878 to 1918. The Borough Council, on this showing, felt able to provide ratepayers with more ambitious entertainment than could be offered by a string quartet in an hotel lounge; Sir Dan Godfrey was engaged to conduct a symphony orchestra in the Winter Garden. All along the South Coast the boom was so good that nothing could restrain municipalities, mostly run by local businessmen, from permitting the profitable destruction of the natural resources on which their prosperity was based. They cheerfully watched whilst their cliffs and downs were devoured by bricks and mortar, and they improvidently piped growing volumes of sewage into the sea, the healing virtues of which were advertised on every railway station.

Further Reading

Singer and Underwood, *Short History of Medicine*
Drummond and Wilbraham, *The Englishman's Food*
A. Hern, *The Seaside Holiday*
Digby and Waterhouse, *The Café Royal*
D. Feilding, *The Duchess of Jermyn Street*

VI

Life in the Country

In 1906, when William Willet, a Chelsea builder, proposed that in the spring clocks should be put back one hour, it was indeed a sign of the times. His Daylight Saving Society, founded two years later, received considerable support, though it did not achieve its aims until after the outbreak of war. Inconvenient as it was for men working on the land to begin their day so early, they no longer represented more than 12 per cent of employed males in England and Wales, according to the census of 1901. This minority lived and worked in two broadly defined areas; in the arable counties of the Midlands, East Anglia and South-East England; and in the grazing counties west of a line drawn from the Pennines through Wiltshire into Dorset, but including also Northumberland, Durham and the North and West Ridings of Yorkshire.

Although wool had been affected, it was the wheat and barley of the arable areas that had been worst hit by the fall in agricultural prices in the last quarter of the nineteenth century. Between 1870 and 1914 the national corn area declined by 30 per cent while the permanent grassland almost doubled. In 1870 arable products had made up about 50 per cent of the national agricultural product; by 1914 their contribution had dwindled to 20 per cent. When war came, exposing the dense population to the threat of starvation, Britain was importing one-half of all food consumed, including three-quarters of the grain for bread. The social and economic implications of the repeal of the Corn Laws had at last come home to roost. Joseph Chamberlain's famous speech at Birmingham in May

111

1903 may have sounded the first trumpet-call for tariff reform, but it would be a long time yet before the Protectionists could go over to the offensive.

Meanwhile, the British farming community was at the mercy of technological revolution. Mechanical harvesters and multi-furrow ploughs, still drawn by great teams of horses and mules, were sweeping across the fertile plains of North America. Steamships were bringing the produce to these shores at prices with which no British farmer could compete. If he switched his production to butcher's meat, his steps were dogged by cheap refrigerated cargoes from Argentina, Australia and New Zealand. If he turned to pig meat and dairy produce, Danish bacon and butter and cheese and margarine from the Netherlands ate into his profits. The farmers who survived best were those who specialized, adapting themselves to the local soil, rainfall and, above all, to the demands of industrial concentrations of population with rising purchasing power. Some became market-gardeners, some fruit farmers; many more went in for milk production. Here technology came to their aid. Although milking-machines made little headway before 1914, the cream-separator had already begun to turn dairying into an industry. There were still old-fashioned dairymaids to be seen with their plungers in the butter-churn, but their mechanical aids were no longer restricted to the lever that worked the cheese-press. Fresh milk and vegetables for the breakfast- and dinner-tables of city-dwellers came to the aid of farmers who showed themselves adaptable.

More important than mechanization of the dairy was the network of railways, carrying the milk-churns into the heart of the cities. As roads improved to accommodate the motor lorry, more farmers found themselves within reach of the station. The Great Western Railway brought milk to London from as far away as 130 miles; with an ever-rising demand, the London retail price for milk remained constant for 20 years up to 1914. Milk was becoming safer to drink. Although pasteurization was not made obligatory during the Edwardian period, standards of hygiene were rising as more dairymen and consumers grew aware of the part milk could play in the spread of typhoid and tuberculosis. It is mainly dairying that explains the gradual increase in the cattle population of England and Wales between 1900 and 1914. During the same period the sheep population fell, in spite of the continuing trend from arable to grassland. The decline was most marked in the arable counties, where sheep-grazing had been an essential element both in crop rotation and in fertilizing the soil. As the sheep moved north and west across the Trent and the Severn, the shepherd in his traditional smock was becoming rarer.

From about 1906 farm income was rising and there was a gradual increase in rents; but the economic and social changes brought about partly by the long depression and partly by legislation had come to stay. Changes on the land are notoriously slow and it had taken the second half of the nineteenth century for the landed interest to adjust itself to the repeal of the Corn Laws and the impact of change in foreign parts. The economic primacy of the landed interest had gone and the value of land had declined. It was inevitable that the relationships of land-owner, farmer and labourer should be affected and it was, of course, the last mentioned who was least able to withstand the economic consequences.

In some areas the labourer had also suffered as a result of nineteenth-century enclosures, which touched the whole structure of rural life. It was on the common lands that the agricultural community had grazed a cow, kept geese and hens, collected faggots, cut turf and tethered the donkey which drew the small cart in which produce was marketed. To the farmers the income from these sources may have seemed marginal, but it was the margin on which the security of humble villagers rested. In particular, it was the safeguard against their being carried off in old age to the workhouse. The declining demand for agricultural labour in the depression hit day-labourers all the harder because they could no longer save against such a crisis. Not until old age pensions were intro-duced in 1908 could old people look forward to spending their last years in the cottages in which they had been reared. Flora Thompson has described their feelings.

113

Ploughing

When the Old Age Pensions began, life was transformed for
. . . aged cottagers. They were relieved of anxiety. They were
suddenly rich. Independent for life! At first when they went
to the Post Office to draw it, tears of gratitude would run
down the cheeks of some, and they would say as they picked
up their money, 'God bless that Lloyd George . . . and God
bless you, miss!' and there were flowers from their gardens
and apples from their trees for the girl who merely handed
them the money.

The lower stratum of the rural community had been lifted up
by the State, not by its traditional helpers—squire and parson.
This tended to undermine the ancient hierarchy, which had
meant, at its best, the interdependence of all elements. The
gradations still remained from squire, parson, yeoman
farmer, bailiff, miller, stonemason, saddler, thatcher, farm
servant down to the lad scaring crows; but the obligations of
reciprocity on which the pyramid was based were giving way.
Many squires continued to succour their dependants and some
who did not were themselves victims of harsh economic facts. Not
all parsons failed their rural parishioners; but enough did to fill
the Methodist chapels. It is not a coincidence that Joseph Arch,
Ashby of Tysoe, George Edwards and other reformers were

Methodists. One of the hymns sung on Sundays at Edwards's open-air meetings began with the verse:

Wife, I have found the Labour Church
And worshipped there today;
It's not like those so long we've known
Where parsons preach for pay.
But one that's built of human love
To bless the human race,
No church that 'ere before it stood
Filled so divine a place.

Employment on the land fell by 18 per cent between 1881 and 1911 and this affected building in the 'closed' villages, where there was one landowner or, at most, two or three. Unless landlords were of a philanthropic disposition, or drew wealth from sources other than land, as at Woburn and Lockinge, they built no new cottages and undertook as few repairs as possible. Farmers drew upon labour reserves in 'open' villages. In some villages in both categories cottages at the turn of the century were no better than hovels and several families might have to make do with one outdoor privy. Large families often had to crowd into a cottage with a pantry and one downstairs room, most of which would be filled by the kitchen fire and oven and a big deal table. Upstairs there would be two bedrooms with ceilings so low that the window-sill was almost on the floor and there was scarcely space for an illuminated text above the head of the bed. When overcrowding in a village became intolerable, there was no remedy except to leave for the town or emigrate; it was usually the more vigorous and enterprising who did so, thus further impoverishing the standards of village life.

Not all farm workers, of course, fared as ill as the day-labourer, who was at the mercy of the seasons and the market, as well as the caprice of his employer. Men with skills, such as carters, wagoners, thatchers, shepherds and cowmen, were taken on by the year, though annual hiring fairs were dying out. They would live in the farmer's house or in 'tied cottages'. It was a hard life and a stockman might have to work as much as five hours on a Sunday; but there was extra at times of lambing and calving. Inevitably the weight of the depression lay most heavily on the lowest paid and least skilled labourers. At the end of the nineteenth century many of them, especially in the South and East, were earning no more than 10*s*.–12*s*. a week. A rather higher level prevailed in the North, where the depression had been less severe and industry offered more competition for labour.

At such low wages the problem of feeding a family was acute; extra money earned at harvest had to provide boots for the winter. Clothing could sometimes be supplemented from the cast-offs of the manor or vicarage. Staple diet was bread, potatoes and tea. Even at 2*d*. a pint beer was a luxury. Except for an occasional rook and rabbit pie, the only meat supply came from the pig-sty. Every family aimed to keep a pig; it was bought early in the year and fattened for killing in late autumn. Head, feet and chitterlings—nothing went to waste. Villagers formed Pig Clubs to help one another with the purchase of the piglet and to provide insurance against its untimely death.

For fresh vegetables the landless cottager was dependent on being granted an allotment. The resistance shown by farmers in many parts of the country, even where land was readily available, contributed to agricultural discontent. In some areas land was parcelled out in allotments of 10 poles (about 300 square yards) at 2*s*. 6*d*. a year. This was not a princely allocation; but, if it had been made in all areas where demand had developed in the nineteenth century, it would have taken some of the heat out of the agitation fostered in rural districts by the itinerant Red Vans of the Land Restoration League, in which Christian Socialists were joined with Henry Georgists. Linked to the demand for allotments was the movement sponsored by Jesse Collins's Rural Labourers' League, which became the Rural League in 1910. It campaigned vigorously for an England of yeoman peasants, each with a holding of 50 acres. This ideal was buried in an almost mythical past; in any case land grants were useless without the capital to build a farmhouse and equip it. The Small Holdings Act of 1908 gave Local Councils power to acquire land, but this power was very sparingly used up to 1914.

By the end of the nineteenth century Joseph Arch's attempt to unionize agricultural workers had foundered in dissension and depression. The man who took up the torch was another labouring man, George Edwards. His success was the more remarkable in that he was already 56 when he yielded to the entreaties

A cottage in Essex

of ill-paid labourers in Norfolk, where he was himself working. By July 1906 he had collected £10 from well-wishers and organized a meeting at North Walsham, at which the Eastern Counties Agricultural Labourers' and Smallholders' Union was launched. The meeting, including tea for the delegates, cost £11, so the new union started with a deficit of £1. For his first year's work as Secretary, Edwards received 13*s.* a week. He worked at his home at Gresham, with his niece doing the correspondence, and averaged 100 miles a week on his bicycle, travelling from place to place. By the end of the year he had opened 49 branches. It was a strenuous life. 'Still,' as he wrote in his autobiography, 'I do not regret the sacrifice I made in the interest of humanity.'

The farmers of East Anglia did not at all appreciate his sacrifice. Branch secretaries were intimidated and threatened with eviction and Edwards himself was assaulted on one occasion by the son of a local farmer. The police broke up meetings on the pretext of obstruction and in 1909, when the first organized strike occurred, the local magistrates imposed £5 fines on a group of strikers alleged to have attacked 'blacklegs', although no evidence was forthcoming that a hand had been laid on one of them. In the five years up to the outbreak of war the Farmers' Federation never once agreed to meet officials of the Union to discuss settlement of disputes.

The difficulty and delay in organizing farm labourers, at a time when industrial unions had everywhere leaped ahead, arose in part from the long tradition of manor and village as elements in the community of the soil. To withhold his labour was foreign to the nature of the countryman; to respect those accustomed to direct his work was a deeply ingrained habit of mind. Even after the Act of 1894 had set up elected District and Parish Councils labouring men often failed to exert the weight of numbers and allowed the gentry to dominate meetings, as they had done in the days of the Vestry. It has been calculated that only 470 houses were built in England and Wales by Rural District Councils between 1909 and 1913.

Nevertheless, progress was made. By 1912 wages in Dorset and East Anglia still averaged no more than 15s. 3d. to 15s. 6d. a week, but in Glamorganshire and most of the North the rate was nearly £1. Need for the Foresters, the 'Sick and Divvies' and similar benefit clubs had declined with the introduction of National Health Insurance. Lord Ernle summed up the advance made by the labourers since 1884:

Most men of the class are still poorly paid; many are precariously employed and poorly housed; among all, poverty is chronic and, though destitution is certainly rare, the dread of it is seldom absent. But, generally speaking, labourers in 1912 are better paid, more regularly employed, better housed, better fed, better clothed. They are better educated and more sober. Their hours of work are shorter.

At the opposite end of the social scale the connection of the aristocracy with the land, on which their wealth and political power had rested, was becoming more tenuous. At the turn of the century it was estimated that over 75 per cent of all agricultural land was farmed by tenants. After 1894 estate duty was levied on land and heirs to property were sometimes obliged to sell, so giving tenants a chance to purchase at the depreciated prices resulting from the depression. A series of Acts passed in the latter part of the nineteenth century, often codifying local custom, loosened the grip of family entails and allowed life-tenants to sell one part of the estate in order to improve another part or, indeed, the house itself. Installation of heating and electric light was regarded after 1905 as legitimate improvement. The major change in the relationship between the landowner and his tenants was brought about by a series of Agricultural Holding Acts, which between 1875 and 1908 gave the tenant much greater security of tenure, freed him from the landowner's direction as to how he should farm and assured him at the end of his tenancy of compensation for improvements. Most expressive of the changing relationship was, perhaps, the provision in the Act of 1906 that the tenant must be compensated for any damage to his crops caused by winged game which only the landlord had the right to kill. At this time farmers were increasingly using barbed-wire, in spite of the objections of Masters of Foxhounds. 'The dethronement of the squirearchy', prophesied 30 years earlier, was at last taking place. In 1908 Colin Campbell, a Scottish farmer settled in Lincolnshire, founded the National Farmers' Union; voting

The hunt meeting outside the Harewood Arms in 1908

rights were significantly restricted to owner-occupiers and tenant-farmers.

The owners of the great houses reacted to their changing circumstances as the individualists they were. Some sold out to the new 'Beer peers' and other industrialists. The fourth Marquess of Ailesbury wished to sell Tottenham Park in Savernake Forest to Lord Iveagh; but his heir, who was his uncle, went to law to prevent the house from passing to 'a mere upstart merchant, a *nouveau riche* Irishman'. When the fifth Marquess succeeded, he let the big house and lived in a smaller one whilst debts were being paid off. By the time he died in 1911 the estate was solvent. The Earl of Verulam let Gorhambury and the shooting for a few years; but his chief remedy for falling farm rents was to accept Director's fees in the City and transfer part of his capital from land to stocks and shares. This practice became increasingly widespread and opened an economic gap between forward-looking and moneyed members of the land-owning class and the old-fashioned squires, who clung to their family acres. The heavy sales of land which began about 1910 have often been ascribed to fear of the radical policies of Lloyd George with his rhetorical charges that 'Labourers have diminished, game has tripled'. But many of those who sold were glad to find a political pretext for a canny diversification of their investments. Nineteen noble estates were wholly or in part up for sale in 1912, at a time when no legislative assault on great landowners was impending.

For those who were cushioned, at least temporarily, against change and decay, time seemed to stand still, as it did for Sebastian on the roof of Chevron (Knole).

Acres of red-brown roof surrounded him, heraldic beasts

carved in stone sitting at each corner of the gables. Across the great courtyard the flag floated red and blue and languid from a tower. Down in the garden, on a lawn of brilliant green, he could see the sprinkled figures of his mother's guests, some sitting under the trees, some strolling about; he could hear their laughter and the tap of the croquet mallets.

They had never had it so good and the Indian Summer could not last. 'The house was really as self-contained as a little town; the carpenter's shop, the painter's shop, the forge, the sawmill, the hot-houses, were there to provide whatever might be needed at a moment's notice.'

The whole elaborate structure depended on an abundance of labour, especially domestic help. There was, of course, no liberty, equality or fraternity below stairs; the hierarchial order observed in high society was faithfully mirrored by those who served it. The housekeeper and butler would have the honoured places at table, followed by the valets and ladies' maids; other servants could take the lower places and all would be waited on by the kitchen-maid and scullery-maid, who formed the lowest rungs of the indoor establishment. If guests were staying in the house, their valets and ladies' maids were dovetailed into the precedence of the servants' hall according to the relative

Two reapers at work, 1907

importance of their masters and mistresses. But there were termites in the venerable woodwork; young men were leaving the carpenter's shop to become mechanics; 'tweenies' were going off to work in factories. Their grandchildren would walk the polished floors as day-tourists.

Liberated from the dead hand of traditionally minded landowners, farmers were freer to make innovations that the age demanded. One of the most successful pioneers was George Baylis, who at the end of the nineteenth century was farming 3,440 acres in Berkshire; by 1914 he had increased his acreage to 10,000. He raised no livestock and used only artificial manures to fertilize his fields, on which he grew grain and hay. In the North farmers were helped by a discovery made at Cockle Park, which had been leased by Northumberland County Council in 1896 for experimentation and teaching. It was found that basic slag, which was abundantly available, encouraged growth of white clover, which has high feed value. The rising cost of growing swedes and turnips led to the introduction of sugar-beet and the first modern factory was started in 1912 at Cantley in Norfolk. Inspectors of the Board of Agriculture were active in trying to prevent disease in potatoes; Bordeaux mixture was one of the most effective sprays brought into use in this period. No remedy was found for wart disease, which came in from North America in 1905, but progress was made with varieties which proved immune. In 1914 a Wart Testing Station was set up by the Board at Ormskirk in Lancashire.

Technology, which had menaced the livelihood of the farmer, came to the aid of those who were prepared to abandon the old methods. In the later Victorian era mechanical reapers, hay-mowing machines and the like came into general use, although they were still horse-drawn. Steam had been used not only to drive stationary machines, but also for ploughing; traction engines, sited on each side of the field, drew the ploughs across by cable. Itinerant mechanics accompanied threshing-machines and sowing-drills, which toured the rural areas. Local deficiencies in the labour force, due to the flight from the land, could be made good by use of machines. Traction engines lacked mobility, however, and their great weight often caused them to be bogged down. In 1902 Dan Albone of Biggleswade produced the first petrol-driven tractor, the Ivel, and in the following year he launched a company to manufacture them. It was not until tractors came into general use after the war that combine-harvesters became a familiar feature of larger farms.

The Ivel tractor, 1902

Use of machinery for ploughing and sowing was regarded with a good deal of scepticism by conservative farmers; the failure of the machines to make excrement was thought to be an incurable disadvantage. But use of simple machines for reaping and mowing meant that farmers could begin reaping as soon as the crop was ready and finish before it was over-ripe, which would otherwise have been impossible without employing a very large labour force. Moreover, machines were cheaper. George Sturt in his diary for late July 1906 records, 'The price mentioned for hand-reaping yesterday was 7s. 6d. per acre. At Mytchett they are firm believers in machinery, and it was pointed out that this price compared ill with the cost of cutting by machine, for with one horse a man can cut five to seven acres a day.' But Sturt betrays where his sympathies lie by wistfully speculating that 'meadow grass grows better after the scythe than after the mowing machine'.

Sturt was well aware, of course, that his own business was in danger. He reports with disapproval how 'men may be seen scrambling new bodies of motor-cars together at top speed . . . with no regard to fine finish of workmanship . . .'. He contrasts this with the care and delight of one of his own workmen, who has an 'artistic eye for the curves of a cart-spoke'. In the same spirit his blacksmith, 'old Will Hammond . . . filed and punched little old archaic patterns in his otherwise finished "front staves" of wagons'. He depicts Will Hammond as belonging to a

Women loading the farm wagons with hay at Lockinge, Berkshire

generation without a future. 'His hands, with the smith's black-
ness begrimed into them unwashably, were thin and bony and
misshapen from 50 years of work for my family.' Sturt and other
thoughtful contemporaries were perhaps less worried about the
gradual disappearance of carters, harness-makers and the like
than they were about the impoverishment of village life that was
accompanying these changes.

A people strangely without even the folk arts are many
labouring-class women, or without even the aspirations for
them. The old cottar pursuits have dropped away from their
lives, because the old opportunities are gone, and they can
get their bread and light and firing and clothes at a shop; and
little to replace the loss seems to have come into their lives.

Among the folk arts that were vanishing Sturt includes cooking,
needlework, preserving and other household duties, which fitted
into the rhythm of the changing seasons.

With the peasant-life, most of the meaning has gone out of
our English landscape and, for me, half of the charm. . . . If
the peasant life was narrow and void of aspirations, at least it
clung to the countryside with a more faithful love than ours
. . . the peasantry nestled in their valleys; more at home there

—tied, subservient as they were to the soil and the seasons among the hills—than we can conceive, who but make a sort of toy and harlot of the beautiful country—keeping it to ourselves, or selling it, without true understanding.

Living as he did on the border of Surrey and Hampshire, Sturt was intensely conscious of the expropriation of the countryside by moneyed people with an urban background; tyrannical as some of the old squires may have been, it was a tyranny that the villager, paying no more than 1*s*. 6*d*. or 2*s*. a week for his cottage, could endure and even understand. Moreover, he was necessary to his employer and unlikely to be evicted. The new men, 'the villa-people', however, were moving in and closing footpaths, and putting up notices that trespassers would be prosecuted.

A Mr Croker Stuart (who bought his house across the valley about 18 months ago and has enlarged it, etc.) secured three of the Smith Wright cottages neighbouring his own place. It was told me, at the time, that his object was to dispossess the present tenants in favour of a more respectable variety; and I could well believe it—for he has the blackguard look and walk and cigar-smoke of a retired publican or bookmaker trying to do the 'gentleman at his little place in the country'. . . . Barney Edwards, in one of these cottages, has a week's notice to quit; the cottage being wanted for Mr Croker Stuart's gardener.

Villages on the fringe of towns found themselves turning into satellites. Traditional loyalty to the village store faltered; a wider variety of goods could be got in the market town. Flora Thompson has described the process of change:

Candleford Green was at that time a separate village. In a few years it was to become part of Candleford. Already the rows of villas were stretching out towards it; but as yet the green with its spreading oak with the white-painted seats, its roofed-in well with the chained bucket, its church spire

Morris dancers c. 1900

soaring out of trees, and its clusters of old cottages, was untouched by change.

Trade and specialization were splitting the organic life of rural communities. Country folk who for centuries had depended on their own mill, brewery, blacksmith and shoemaker had turned to alien sources of supply. The village windmill could not compete with flour ground by steam at the great ports; the country maltster was helpless before the mechanized production of the city breweries. Sometimes small adjustments to the new trends could be made. Miss Thompson records how venturesome smiths would paint above the shop door, 'Motor Repairs a Speciality'. But she also traces how within a few years the local carpenter, William, his son and grandson vanished from the village that had known them so long. The youngest William joined up in the Boer War and found a grave on the veld.

Soon after, the middle William died suddenly while working at his bench, and his father followed him next winter. Then the carpenter's shop was demolished to make way for a builder's showroom with baths and tiled fireplaces and w.c. pans in the window, and only the organ in church and pieces of good woodwork in houses remained to remind those who had known them of the three Williams.

It was not only the old familiar trades and crafts that were dying out; the entertainments that the villagers made for themselves were being replaced by something synthetic. Although many villagers still rang Grandsire Triples and other peals in their own church on Sundays, the practice of touring the district to ring bells in other belfries was becoming less frequent. The 'Mummers', who called at country houses and acted their traditional plays, especially at Christmas, were not what they used to be; the younger generation was dropping out. Kenneth

Grahame in December 1908 found the Mummers in the Thames valley a disappointment. 'Hardly any of the good old "St George and the Dragon" play left. Instead, cheap comic songs from the London music halls.' If there was Morris dancing, it was usually a self-conscious revival.

Those young men who wished to remain on the land were more interested in the new possibilities of having water and electric light than they were in the preservation of the customs of the past. Candles and thatch had never gone well together; in a dry summer, when it was impossible to collect rainwater, some villages, especially those on high chalk, suffered severely. The case is recorded in Hampshire of a gardener's wife who for six weeks made her husband a new shirt each week, because there was no water in which to wash the dirty ones. Picturesque old cottages had no charm for the young farm workers and they moved out, if they could, abandoning the home of their forbears. Flora (Laura)Thompson recalls one in decay:

After they had gone, their old house stood empty for years. The population of the hamlet was falling and none of the newly married couples cared for the thatched roof and stone floors. . . . When Laura visited the hamlet just before the [First World] War, the roof had fallen in, the yew hedge had run wild and the flowers were gone, excepting one pink rose which was shedding its petals over the ruin. To-day, all has gone, and only the limy whiteness of the soil in a corner of a ploughed field is left to show that a cottage once stood there.

It had been recognized in the nineteenth century by John Ruskin and others that rural communities had a cultural life of their own, which was fast disappearing. The loss to the national culture as a whole became increasingly manifest as standards of Victorian taste continued to decline and mass production was applied to the domestic and other artefacts which craftsmen had formerly fashioned for themselves and their immediate circle. The reaction of William Morris and the Aesthetic School had been a retreat into the past; handlooms and spinning-wheels were dusted and brought back into use and themes from the

Middle Ages and the Celtic Twilight came briefly into fashion. By the end of the century, however, the vagaries of Art for Art's Sake had grown more and more extravagant and decorative; patterns, based on the lily or the peacock's feather, were increasingly stylized. It was clear that if salvation was to be found for the crude materialism of industrial civilization, it would not come from 'the greenery-yallery, bats in the gallery, foot-in-the-grave young man' of the eighties and nineties.

It seemed to some reformers that socialism held the answer; others believed it could be found in a return to religion; a few tried to combine both remedies. The religious school of thought, accepting as dogma the antithesis between science and religion, ascribed to science the evils of technology, as expressed in industrial slums, and placed its hopes in a religious revival. One of the eddies on this stream was represented by The New Crusade, which took as its motto: 'Simplicitas, Ars, Ardor'. It demanded 'the restoration of Country Life, in place of that of the modern manufacturing town, and of country crafts instead of mechanical industries'. This movement, with its organ of publicity, The Simple Life Press, had its headquarters at Haslemere in Surrey, where there was a Country Church, devoted to a primitive, undogmatic form of Christian worship. Thoreau and Tolstoy were the prophets of the gospel of simplicity.

Another minor current, which merged Christianity with socialism, flowed through rural Essex. It owed its socialism to Frances, Countess of Warwick of Easton Lodge and her near neighbour, H. G. Wells. Christianity was provided by Conrad Noel, who was appointed by Lady Warwick to the living of Thaxted. There he combined High Anglicanism with passionate concern for the wrongs of agricultural workers. His favourite slogan was that of Wat Tyler's fourteenth-century rebellion:

When Adam delved and Eve span,
Who was then the gentleman?

Whilst his wife revived folk-dancing in Thaxted, Conrad Noel promoted the Church Socialist League and was Chairman of the local branch of the National Union of Agricultural Workers. The turn of the century gave voice to echoes of a remoter faith. A thread of pantheism and nature-magic had run through the nineteenth century, finding perhaps its purest expression in Richard Jefferies's *Story of My Heart*. Admirers of Jefferies, like Edward Thomas and W. H. Hudson, found in his attitude to nature a substitute for institutional religion. It seemed to some of their contemporaries that the countryside might offer a cure, as well as a contrast, for the evils of industrialism and materialism. Nature was personified as a lovely woman, ravaged by heartless commercialism and the pursuit of gain. Had she means of avenging herself? The sly, malicious figure of Pan makes his appearance in the books of several writers of the period, notably E. M. Forster, Arthur Machen, Richard Le Gallienne and 'Saki'.

Other writers responded to the desecration of nature with nostalgia for the past. Typical of these is Kenneth Grahame, who had made his name in the nineties with *The Golden Age* and *Dream Days*. His final and best-known work was *The Wind in the Willows*. In all his books there is the feeling of sadness that time, like the river, carries everything away, especially the carefree days of our youth. Change, to which Mr Toad is so responsive, tends to be change for the worse. It is true that the Stoats and Weasels are driven out of Toad Hall and its rightful owner shows himself a reformed character in the last pages of the book; but we all know it cannot last. Social change is the order of the day and the Wild Wooders will be back—this time for good. Grahame's biographer, Peter Green, sums up the atmosphere pervading his work:

It embodies in miniature the whole essence of pre-1914 England—the smooth lawns, the river-picnics, the long, sun-drenched days of idleness, the holidays in Italy, the self-assurance and the stable values. The currents of change and revolution do little more than ruffle the surface of this summer stream: they eddy deep below among the sinuous weeds, unseen, biding their time.

The river, which meanders through *The Wind in the Willows*, was matched on land by the highways and by-ways, which still belonged to the horse and the pedestrian, though their right was

'Diana of the Uplands'

already challenged by the motor car. There grew up a literature of the Open Road, or the Broad Highway, as we should perhaps call it after a novel by Jeffrey Farnol, which was a best-seller in 1910. We find it mirrored in Charles Furse's painting 'Diana of the Uplands', depicting an out-of-doors Edwardian beauty (she was his wife), holding two greyhounds on leash against a wind-swept background. In music, one recalls Frederick Delius's early tone-poem, 'Over the Hills and Far Away', which marvellously evokes the urge to quit the confined life of the great city.

Although the despoilers of the countryside had taken only a few short steps, compared with the giant strides we observe today, the direction in which they were going was already plain. Among those who reacted in a practical way were those who joined together in 1895 to found The National Trust. Octavia Hill and Sir Robert Hunter did much to preserve open spaces within reach of London, such as Epping Forest and the Devil's Punchbowl at Hindhead. Canon Rawnsley was particularly active in the Lake District. A Royal Commission on Ancient Monuments was also set up.

E. M. Forster in a preface written later for a book first published in 1907 wrote:

There was a freshness and out-of-door wildness in those days which the present generation cannot imagine. I am glad I have known our countryside before its roads were too dangerous to walk on and its rivers too dirty to bathe in, before its butterflies and wildflowers were decimated by chemical sprays, before Shakespeare's Avon frothed with detergents and fish floated belly up on the Cam.

The Edwardian period was one in which many people looked on the English countryside with new eyes; some knew it would never be so beautiful again. 'Look thy last on all things lovely . . .', as Walter de la Mare wrote. In pursuit of pleasure, or profit, or prestige, men were fanning out across the land as never before. Mostly they followed the roads and the railways and they brought with them a trail of stucco or roughcast villas with some discreet half-timbering in the upper storey beneath the red tiles. Behind them came the tea-shops and garages and hotels. When the trail of devastation reached the sea, it spread out along the coast, until it came to an estuary, or a marsh, or inaccessible cliffs. It flowed like larva; it had been pent up too long.

Further Reading

Orwin and Whetham, *History of British Agriculture*
Lord Ernle, *English Farming Past and Present*
F. M. L. Thompson, *English Landed Society in the Nineteenth Century*
M. K. Ashby, *Joseph Ashby of Tysoe*
Sir G. Edwards, *From Crow-Scaring to Westminster*
G. E. Evans, *Ask the Fellows Who Cut the Hay*
F. Thompson, *Lark Rise to Candleford*

VII

Childhood, Youth and Education

The attitude of parents towards their children born towards the end of the nineteenth century was not, on the whole, a healthy one: it tended to vacillate between an undiscerning faith in childish innocence and an equally misguided determination to treat disobedient children as sons of Belial. Both extremes were based on ignorance of the child's nature; it is as if the great majority of Victorian parents forgot what it was like to be a child. Nor were opportunities of observing the behaviour of their young as frequent as a modern parent would suppose. Among the poor, long hours of work abbreviated family life, especially in the towns, and childhood itself was cut short by the early beginning of wage-earning, even after the worst abuses of juvenile employment had been remedied. In the middle and upper classes a nurse and later a governess took charge of the young and in many households even the mother only saw her children at certain hours. There were fathers who, when they wished, like the Creator, to walk in the garden in the cool of the evening, caused a handbell to be rung as a warning to the children to make themselves scarce.

It was easy to be sentimental or stern towards children whom the parent seldom saw; to enter with understanding into their lives and problems was more difficult. Kenneth Grahame dubbed the grown-ups the Olympians, because of their remoteness from the young. 'The estrangement was fortified by an abiding sense of injustice, arising from the refusal of the

Olympians ever to defend, to retract, to admit themselves in the wrong, or to accept similar concessions on our part.' Rosamund Lehmann, recalling a rather later period, strikes a similar note.

No grown-up, in my personal experience, ever said sorry to a child in those days. None, in the event of inability to answer a question, ever confessed to simple ignorance. As for such subjects as birth, death, physical and sexual functions, these were taboo, and invested with an aura of murk, shame, guilt, suggestiveness and secrecy.

Much of the blame for this state of affairs must be laid at the door of the paterfamilias; in all ranks of society his word was law. In middle-class families, in which Puritanism was especially strong, religion took a heavy toll of the exuberance of youth. Much of what a later generation has been willing to write off as animal spirits was sombrely ascribed to original sin, which required to be pitilessly reproved. Sons were consigned at an early age to schools at which the birch was known to be an inescapable part of the curriculum. 'The word had gone forth, the school had been selected; the necessary sheets were hemming and Edward was the designated and appointed victim.' It was the beginning of the process that would transform the carefree child of Kenneth Grahame's story into a staid young man who might, like Grahame himself, marry an unsatisfactory wife and become Secretary to the Governor of the Bank of England.

If gentlemen's sons were exposed to the rigours of school life and subjected there to the customary floggings, a poor and orphaned child could not hope to fare better. In 1896 Charlie Chaplin was consigned to the Hanwell School for Orphans and Destitute Children. He gives the following description of the punishment meted out to the young offender:

For minor offences a boy was laid across the long desk, face downwards, feet strapped and held by a sergeant, then another sergeant pulled the boy's shirt out of his trousers and over his head, then pulled his trousers tight. Captain

Hindrum, a retired Navy man weighing about two hundred pounds, with one hand behind him, the other holding a cane as thick as a man's thumb and about four feet long, stood poised, measuring it across the boy's buttocks. Then slowly and dramatically he would lift it high and with a swish bring it down across the boy's bottom. The spectacle was terrifying, and invariably a boy would fall out of rank in a faint.

It was not to be expected that the new century would at once lead to a new approach to the problems of childhood; but if the process was slow the measures introduced by the Edwardians were practical ones and operated from birth. Infant mortality had reached its peak in 1899 and many of the deaths were known to be preventable. A beginning was made in 1902 with the registration of midwives; they were not required to be qualified as nurses, but at least the machinery of control now existed. In 1907 the first Notification of Births Act was passed, although notification did not become general and compulsory until 1915. In the period 1906–1910 infant mortality per 1,000 births fell to 117, as compared with 138 for the preceding five years. The first Nursery School started at Deptford in January 1900 and its inauguration was greeted as the dawn of 'the children's century'. Legislation providing for school meals was adopted in 1906 and in the following year the Board of Education established its own Medical Department and enjoined upon Local Education Authorities the medical inspection of school-children. Special schools for incapacitated children began in 1908. Between 1907 and 1908 Parliament gave some attention to the problems of delinquent children; it was belatedly recognized that it was neither rational nor socially expedient to treat young offenders in the same way as hardened criminals. Herbert Samuel, as Under Secretary of State at the Home Office, was mainly responsible for legislation collectively known as 'The Children's Charter'. Probation Officers and Juvenile Courts were instituted and Borstals were set up to inculcate better habits.

Even this more humane approach to delinquency, however, had primarily a negative character. Just as in the field of medicine doctors were recognizing that prevention was better than cure, so in the juvenile field there were far-sighted men who came to the conclusion that the interest of the individual child and of the State lay in channelling the activity of young people in a healthy direction before anti-social habits were formed. The Church Lads' Brigade and the Boys' Brigade had already made progress along this road and by 1904 the latter claimed a membership of 54,000 in the British Isles.

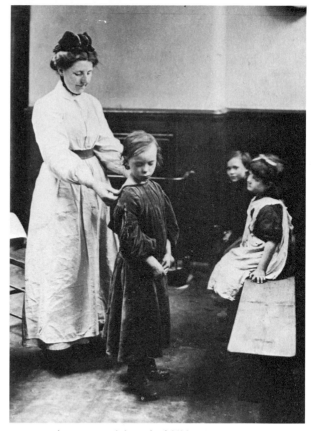

A nurse examining schoolchildren

The movement that captured the imagination of young people all over the world had its genesis not in the slums of Glasgow, like the Boys' Brigade, but within the beleaguered town of Mafeking, where Colonel Baden-Powell and his Chief of Staff, Major Lord Edward Cecil, had organized the boys to make themselves useful during the siege. The germinal idea lay dormant until April 1904, when Baden-Powell, now Inspector-General of Cavalry, inspected the twenty-first anniversary parade of the Boys' Brigade. He approved of what he saw; but it struck him that the reproduction in miniature of the drill of soldiers could scarcely exercise as strong an appeal to a boy's mind as would an adaption of some of the activities that he had already outlined in his manual *Aids to Scouting*. His aim was to lead the young people out of the towns, with their squalor and temptations, towards the healthy

135

Westminster Children's Court, 1910

countryside and coast; to make them active and train them to
use their powers of observation and acquire simple skills. The
age of 'spectator sport' had begun and he had seen, as he put
it, 'thousands of boys and young men, pale, narrow-chested,
hunched-up miserable specimens, smoking endless cigarettes,
numbers of them betting'.

Powerful backing was provided by the newspaper magnate,
C. Arthur Pearson, and the next step led to Brownsea Island in
Poole Harbour, which had been acquired a few years earlier by
a wealthy stockbroker, Charles van Raalte, who was sympa-
thetic to Baden-Powell's aims. There on the sun-baked clay at
the end of July 1907 the first Scout camp was pitched and for
the next ten days the first patrols of Curlews, Ravens, Wolves

and Bulls crawled through the gorse and bracken, raced through the pine trees and gathered in the evening round the camp-fire to listen to the wise words and exciting tales of the 'Hero of Mafeking'. The Union Jack flew from the flag-pole; the boys stood for a prayer before turning in for a night under canvas. Scouting was born.

The new movement answered a need; it was an immediate success. In January 1908, Part I of *Scouting for Boys* was on sale for 4*d*. In May, all six Parts were published in book form at 2*s*. a copy. Soon the weekly, *The Scout*, was also in circulation and by the end of 1908, 110,000 copies were being sold each week. C. B. Fry, the Edwardian ideal of the scholar-athlete, who was preparing boys for a life at sea in the training ship *Mercury*, co-operated with Baden-Powell in organizing an amphibious camp and the Sea Scouts were launched. In the same year, 1909, at the great Scout rally at the Crystal Palace Baden-Powell came upon a small group of girls in white blouses, with floppy sleeves, blue skirts below the knees and black stockings. They had organized themselves; they were the first Girl Guides. The appeal was irresistible and Baden-Powell's sister, Agnes, accepted responsibility for them. The movements spread: broomsticks were hastily improvised to serve as Scout staves and strange symbols began to appear on woodland paths, signifying

Baden-Powell (arrowed) *talking to a group of scouts, 1908*

Girl Guides doing stretcher drill

'Turn left' or 'I have gone home'. By the end of 1910 there were nearly 108,000 Scouts in Britain and Scouting was starting up in the Empire and in Europe. It had all sprung from B.-P.'s original objective: 'To help existing organisations in making the rising generation, of whatever class or creed, into good citizens or useful colonists.'

The middle-class child might join a Scout or Guide camp in the summer, but not at the expense of the annual family holiday by the sea. For privileged children this was indeed a Golden Age. One can still conjure up those halcyon days; stretches of sand uncontaminated by oil slick or the litter of the urban masses; no speedboats to terrorize swimmers, but a peaceful seascape with cliffs of gorse and heather or sandy turf, where a few bungalows were beginning to show but had not yet destroyed the skyline. Friendships would grow up between families in neighbouring tents, or housed in the same boarding-house. Rosamund Lehmann has evoked it in a story recalling her own Edwardian childhood.

> There, as usual, comes the sailing dinghy *Seamew;* the dark boy in a white public school sweater at the tiller; with him the fair pig-tailed girl in a green blazer; brother or sister, or maybe cousins, fortunate pair; and they are hero and heroine of a voluminous Book for Girls about a jolly pair of boy and girl chums, Jack and Peggy (Pegs), who charter a boat for the hols and have all sorts of adventures. They wave to us; we wave back; romantic moment. Receding, they stay fixed, an illustration, between blue water and blue sky, their crimson sail behind them. Till next summer, next summer . . .

A few philanthropic bodies gave a thought to the vast majority of children, whose parents could not afford a seaside holiday. The Children's Country Holiday Fund was one, and the Pearson Fresh Air Fund also organized outings for poor children. As there were no motor charabancs, the trip, unless short enough to be made in a horse-drawn vehicle, would be made by train and the children would debouch on to the sands of one of the large and rapidly expanding resorts, such as Blackpool, Brighton, Margate, or Clacton; *Punch* had already described the last mentioned as the 'Mentone of the East'. On these more densely populated beaches there would be Pierrots and Punch and Judy shows and donkey-rides and, if charity extended to a penny for the turnstile, there would be a helter-skelter down the pier, and perhaps whelks from a barrow to satisfy young appetites before the return journey to the slums of some industrial town.

The main hope of the poor child, wishing to escape from the insanitary and dispiriting surroundings in which he had been born, lay in education. The foundation of our modern State educational system was laid in 1902, when Balfour's Education Act was passed. It was probably the most momentous piece of legislation enacted by his Government, but the Liberals, mindful of the Non-conformist vote, attacked the measure on the ground that it allowed financial support for denominational private schools. Lloyd George even proposed that his fellow Welsh-Nonconformists should refuse to pay rates in support of the new system. In fact, the Act was timely and far-sighted. From an industrial point of view, Britain could no longer prosper on unskilled labour; from a political point of view, democracy required that the majority of the population should receive enough education to become responsible citizens.

Schoolchildren on an outing to the Shirley Hills, 1912

A drawing class

The new Act, for which the Permanent Secretary of the Board of Education, Sir Robert Morant, has been given much of the credit, created a national system of primary and secondary education. Whilst abolishing the old School Boards, however, it wisely kept the principle of local responsibility; Local Education Authorities, based on the Counties, were accordingly set up throughout England and Wales. Common standards were assured by the continued existence of a corps of Inspectors; but the highly centralized French system, with all control vested in the Ministry, was sedulously avoided. It was a decision that nobody has regretted.

The reorganization of education on sound lines did not, of course, solve all problems; the quality of teaching in State Elementary Schools left much to be desired. Half a degree up the social scale from the Elementary School was the Free Church School; it did not follow that the education was better. Here is young Harold Owen, no doubt wearing the Norfolk knickerbocker suit, with stockings and boots and a narrow white collar which, he tells us in *Journey from Obscurity*, was

much in vogue among schoolboys of that period. . . . The other pupils, coming as they did from some of the poorest homes in Birkenhead, were ragged and dirty, always with running noses and often with running sores. . . . We were marshalled into the schoolroom for regulation hours, piped some miserable hymn or the Lord's Prayer and after chanting a multiplication table (I cannot recall any other instruction we were given) we children would sit at our desks in apathetic trances of varying degree. The master in charge sat at his desk, scanning a piece of newspaper in an even more dejected and dispirited manner. . . . We were all cold and hungry. . . .

Even the older Grammar Schools left much to be desired. Sir Reader Bullard describes one in Walthamstow, which was

taken over later by the Education Authority under the Act of 1902, and transferred to a fine new building with playing fields. . . . In 1899, however, the school consisted of a small one-storeyed building with a gravel yard, across the road from an active pickle-factory. The backbone of the school consisted of two masters: neither had a degree, but both were hard workers and good teachers. At the bottom of the school was a large, noisy form. . . . The two top forms (maximum age perhaps just 16) worked in the same room and often together, under an unqualified master who left soon after to become secretary to a firm of dairymen. . . . Because of the openings for office-workers in London, all the top forms studied Pitman's shorthand.

It was not surprising that the teaching profession offered few attractions to the bright student on the threshold of a career. A pupil-teacher in an elementary school had four years' training from the age of 14. He would begin by working five and a half days a week for a wage of 6s., attending secondary school courses on half-days. It was arduous and not very rewarding, but at 18, if he passed matriculation, he would qualify as an assistant master, earning £70 a year. This is how Sir Reader Bullard describes the first step in a teaching career that was later diverted to the Consular Service and ended in the British Embassy in Teheran.

I was posted to a school in the poorest corner of Walthamstow. There were no official school meals then, but a benevolent

Squirrel Nutkin

society ran a soup kitchen to provide a midday meal for the most needy children. Six meal tickets were allotted to my class, but I had twelve boys who were acknowledged to be in need of them. Every day six of the boys had a soup-kitchen meal, the other boys consumed several slabs each of bread thickly spread with butter which I brought to school with me, my mother and sister helping with the cost.

The children from well-to-do homes had very much less to contend with in their search for knowledge and advancement in their careers. They need never go to school too cold and hungry to concentrate on their lessons; their classrooms were less draughty and less congested and their teachers were likely to have shared the same educational advantages as themselves. Moreover they came from homes well furnished with books. They might well have learned to read with the help of *Benjamin Bunny* by Beatrix Potter, which in October 1904 *Punch* described —rather inadequately, as generations of children must think— as 'a pretty booklet. Suitable as a present.' Older children would read E. Nesbit's *The Railway Children* and would spend long hours browsing in *The Children's Encyclopaedia*, which was brought out by the enterprising Harmsworth Press. *Kim* had recently appeared, and, after 1906, they might be taken by their parents at Christmas to see the fantasy that J. M. Barrie in *Peter Pan* constructed round Kensington Gardens, which had seemed such a prosaic place when Nanny had taken them for a walk there. For a halfpenny the schoolboy could subscribe each week to *Pluck* or *Marvel*, graduating later to *Chums* or *The Boys' Own Paper*.

Books about school life, which in the days of F. Anstey's *Vice Versa* or Dean Farrar's *Eric, or Little by Little* seemed to have been written primarily to amuse or edify grown-ups, had taken a turn for the better with Kipling's famous *Stalky and Co.* (1899) and the novels of E. F. Benson and Hugh Walpole. The Public Schoolboy even found a Laureate in Henry Newbolt, an Old Cliftonian, who declaimed that:

> *For, working days or holidays,*
> *And glad or melancholy days,*
> *They were great days and jolly days*
> *At the best school of all.*

Anyone who believes that the boisterous life of Westward Ho, as depicted by Kipling, is exaggerated would do well to study the Haileybury mutiny of the year 1900. It was touched off by the refusal of the headmaster, Canon Edward Lyttelton, to grant a half-holiday in celebration of the relief of Ladysmith. After taking the wise precaution of first eating their lunch, some 500 boys marched to Hertford, singing 'Rule Britannia' and other patriotic songs. They then marched on to Ware, where the headmaster was said to be playing golf, but failed to make contact with him. Contact was made all right after Chapel that evening, when Lyttelton, who came of a family famous

'Fairies are all more or less in hiding until dusk'

for athletic prowess, proceeded to beat ten selected boys in each house, thus dealing with over 100 before close of play. One boy had padded himself with the Union Jack, but even this example of interested patriotism brought no reprieve.

In a more serious spirit, however, it must be said that in the new century the legacy of Arnold, which has been well summed-up as classics, cricket and Christianity, was proving less and less adequate. For one thing, to teach Greek and Latin intelligibly makes exceptional demands upon the teacher and few could meet them. Sir Llewellyn Woodward records,

I was introduced to the grammar of the classical languages. Hic haec hoc hunc hanc hoc hujus hujus hujus huic huic huic hoc hac hoc. This was how I learned Latin grammar. No wonder that I disliked it. . . . I had no idea why I was learning Greek and Latin. It rarely occurred to me that, once upon a time, Greek and Latin were spoken languages. . . . From the first to the last hour of my schooldays I was not given any instruction in the physical or biological sciences. . . .

The Public Schools, by and large, were strongholds of educational complacency and conservatism because Oxford and Cambridge were likewise. At Cambridge remarkable scientific work was being done; but until 1907 the demand for physics and chemistry for the whole University was being catered for by five lecture-rooms and a teaching staff of 46. There were, of course, enlightened dons and schoolmasters who recognized the need to rethink the nineteenth-century concept of the aim of education. Then, as now, the root question was whether education should seek to produce a man who could use in his career the knowledge he had acquired, or whether the object was to train a mind and character which would respond afterwards to the stresses of life. If we criticize the Edwardians for allowing this important debate to degenerate, as it tended to do, into a stereotyped argument about the benefits of a classical, as against a scientific and more modern education, we must remember how difficult it was for them to envisage the environment for which young people were being prepared. Their world was changing with bewildering rapidity and the wisest could not see what the future might hold.

The Late Victorian and Edwardian periods had been marked by innovations which were to have as profound an effect on social and economic life in Britain as had those of the Industrial Revolution. The internal combustion engine and the application of electric power radically altered transportation and men were already looking confidently to the conquest of the air. Wireless and the telegraphic cable had likewise transformed communications and brought people into a changed relationship to one another. Medical science had elucidated the mysteries of bacteriology, antisepsis and the ductless glands, whilst the psychologists had thrown open to inspection the haunted house of the Unconscious. Experiments in the constitution of matter, notably those of Lord Rutherford, disclosed vistas as startling as those once foreshadowed by Galileo and the heliocentrists.

It would indeed be surprising if Edwardian schools and universities had at once succeeded in domesticating these manifold discoveries and adapting the teaching syllabus to them. They still conceived it their duty primarily to turn out men who would administer their estates and serve their country as politicians, soldiers or colonial administrators. The logical weakness of the traditionalists' argument was in assuming that only classical studies could provide the required mental discipline. This point of view is well expressed in the following

The Fourth of June at Eton

extract from a letter written in 1908 by a much-loved Eton master, H. E. Luxmoore:

I had a letter from Cromer enclosing a passage from one of his speeches praising the old 'public school boy' type as efficient for government and work (Harold Perry turned it into Latin prose). I do think something is gained in that direction by the 'Humanities' which is lost in modern and easier and looser studies.

What Luxmoore meant by modern studies is made plain by an earlier letter, in which he comments on a speech by Lord Lytton criticizing the Eton curriculum.

Of course what lies behind it all is that they feel they did not learn the things they are using now. Geography, English, History and the like. . . . All we say is you came to us to be made an educated, capable, good man, and you are so. . . . French is one of those 'utility' subjects which are not real education, and to which some seem to want to reduce all our work.

In an earlier period T. H. Huxley had used his position as a Governor of Eton to install a laboratory in which his grandson, Julian, later studied biology; but it continued to be known as 'Huxley's Folly'.

The other obsession of the Public Schools, which was beginning to attract criticism, was their belief in team games as a means of training character and assuring physical fitness. This traditional belief was perpetuated by giving high marks to applicants for teaching posts who had an athletic record and could coach in games. Sir Henry Newbolt, that eminent Laudator Ludorum, convinced himself and many others that the voice that rallied the ranks when 'the Gatling's jammed and the Colonel dead' would have been silent but for the fact that the junior officer a few years before had survived that last hour of play in the Close despite 'a bumping pitch and a blinding light'. There was never any very satisfactory evidence for this hypothesis. Its principal effect was to create at the Public Schools an aristocracy of athletes, whose predilections and prejudices severely discouraged learning.

The worship of sport was bad enough; the hero-worship of schoolboy athletes was worse.

Playing the game

Nowhere has the tendency been more succinctly described than in Kipling's story, *The Brushwood Boy.*

Ten years at an English public school do not encourage dreaming. Georgie won his growth and chest measurement, and a few other things, which did not appear in the bills, under a system of cricket, football and paper-chases from four to five days a week, which provided for three lawful cuts of a ground-ash if any boy absented himself from these entertainments. . . . At last he blossomed into full glory as head of the school, ex-officio captain of the games; head of his house, where he and his lieutenants preserved discipline and decency among 70 boys from 12 to 17 . . . the school was not encouraged to dwell on its emotions, but rather to keep in hard condition, to avoid false quantities and to enter the army direct, without the help of the expensive London crammer, under whose roof young blood learns too much . . . his training had set the public school mask upon his face and had taught him how many were the 'things no fellow can do'. By virtue of the same training he kept his pores open and his mouth shut.

Keeping the pores open was much recommended as an aid to

a chaste life by muscular Christians, who were influential in schools and universities at this period. A majority of headmasters at both Preparatory and Public Schools were in Holy Orders and at some of the latter promotion to housemaster was even made conditional upon becoming ordained. It was believed to inspire confidence in parents and to be a safeguard against homosexuality. Whether this belief was justified no statistics now relate; but as far as religious instruction is concerned the system has not attracted in retrospect any large number of supporters. Robert Graves has recorded of a preparatory school which he attended in Wales: 'Here I had my first beating. The headmaster, a parson, caned me on the bottom because I learned the wrong collect one Sunday by mistake. I had never before come upon forcible training in religion.' Graves, who came of a very religious family, has also observed: 'My religious training developed in me a great capacity for fear —I was perpetually tortured by the fear of hell—a superstitious conscience and a sexual embarrassment from which I have found it very difficult to free myself.'

Even before the nineteenth century drew to a close, discerning men had come to see that the ideals of Dr Arnold were not enough. One of the pioneers was Cecil Reddie, who founded the first of the New Schools at Abbotsholme in Derbyshire. One of Reddie's assistant masters was J. H. Badley, who had been head boy of Arnold's old House at Rugby and knew all about the shortcomings of the Public Schools. In 1893 he started his own school, Bedales, in Sussex; but it was not until six years later that he embarked upon his most thorough-going innovation— coeducation. In this he was much encouraged by his wife, a wholehearted feminist. The experiment succeeded; but there must have been times when this was in doubt. One of the first of the Old Girls recalled many years later: 'On looking back I still have a strong feeling of pride at having been one of the few girls at the Old Bedales. We were not welcomed by the boys . . .' The school began to expand and in 1900 moved to Steep in Hampshire, where new buildings were going up to accommodate the 70 boys and seven girls. The temporary expedients adopted by Badley whilst the buildings were going up must have been a rude shock to a tenderly nurtured boy from a middle-class home. One of them afterwards described the sanitary arrangements.

He advocated a simple form of earth-closet, or rather a line of such. Once, or was it twice?, a week these were scraped out. The headmaster wielded the shovel, and we boys wheeled away the barrows, sometimes swimming to the brim, and a hard task for weaklings like myself. No one dared complain. A tonic hardihood was inculcated in us all.

It was not only the buildings that needed attention; work had also to be done to prepare playing-fields and a swimming-bath. It was part of Badley's new doctrine that his pupils should share in this work for the commonweal and, as team sports were not held in the same high esteem as at traditional Public Schools, afternoons were set aside for manual work. This was at that time another striking innovation. Badley has recorded how in Bedales' earliest years a small boy, who had just been instructed in his task on a muddy afternoon, explained indignantly, 'I can't do that, Sir; I'm a gentleman!' It was Badley's aim to disabuse his pupils of the idea that it was degrading to learn to do something useful with one's hands. Woodwork and metal-work formed part of the curriculum. He tried to give a practical turn to everything that was taught; Shakespeare's plays were acted as well as studied and French and German were taught by the 'direct' method at a time when these languages were grudgingly taught at most traditional public schools and, even so, taught as dead literature and not as living, spoken tongues. If today these changes do not sound very revolutionary, it is in large measure because reforms at Bedales and other New Schools have come to be widely accepted. Other departures from school life, as Badley had known it at Rugby, included the abolition of 'fagging' and the absence of a school chapel; instead simple, non-denominational services were taken by Bradley himself or a member of the staff. All these innovations aroused the misgivings of the conventionally minded, but the school prospered and by 1913 the numbers, including the Junior House, had risen to 200.

The great question of educational reform inevitably touched the Universities, as their entrance requirements, then as now, had a decisive influence on school curricula. Controversy concentrated upon the demand for Greek. On this point, Luxmoore's attitude may be taken as typical of sound conservative opinion. He wrote in 1901:

> . . . The endowed or ancient Schools and Colleges should be fortresses of the humanities but there should be all kinds of more utilitarian and more modern systems at London, Victoria, Birmingham and the like. Therefore I am against relaxing Responsions. But I am very much in favour of raising the standard, and also if a very smart Science or Math man knows no Greek I don't see much harm in letting him in, but I had rather he went to Owens College or Liverpool.

The decision to retain Greek as a compulsory subject at Oxford was, in fact, confirmed in 1904. There was an uneasy feeling, however, that all was not well at England's oldest university and Bishop Gore of Birmingham referred to it as a playground of the idle rich; demands for reform became insistent. In 1907 Curzon was admitted Chancellor by Convocation in full conclave, the first Chancellor to be so admitted since the days of Oxford's Jacobite sympathies. He at once set out to forestall the appointment of a Commission of Inquiry by offering reform from within and two years later proposals were published which silenced the most vociferous critics, without much altering the character of the University. The Oxonian reaction to the efforts of a civic university to move with the times is well illustrated by the following verse in *Punch*, inspired by the news that the University of Manchester was to have a faculty of Commerce and Administration.

> *Two Christchurch men came down the street*
> *Discussing their exams.*
> *Quoth one, 'I'm through in frozen meat*
> *But ploughed again in hams.'*

*'Hard lines!' said Number Two. 'The Dean
Just told me I have taken
An alpha plus in margarine
Although I'm gulfed in bacon.'*

Probably the most valid criticism of Oxbridge, though in Edwardian times it was still muted, was the financial limitation on attendance by scholars of poor parents. There was a way open, but it was an arduous climb over College walls, instead of strolling in through the main gate, which was regarded as the almost automatic privilege of any young man, able to read and write, whose father had trod the same path before him. There were too few scholarships open to all comers; too many closed scholarships offered by Colleges to particular Public Schools. An Oxbridge education in Edwardian times was not very costly; Sir Charles Petrie has estimated that, excluding clothes, vacations and travel, a young man could manage on about £160 a year. Sir Reader Bullard, who was a Student Interpreter at Cambridge in 1906 at the expense of the Foreign Office, has recorded that he 'was rich on £200 a year'. It was not merely a question of money; economic life was ordered on the assumption that a young man from a poor family would begin earning as soon as he could; many parents who had themselves had no more than an Elementary School education wished to see their better educated sons gaining a good wage before age or ill health disabled the father of the family, who would in most cases have girls and younger children to support. In this respect parents also required to be educated.

The restriction of access, broadly speaking, to the upper and middle classes was the more regrettable because many undergraduates failed to profit by their opportunities. Sir Charles Petrie recalls that in 1909 one-quarter of those who matriculated at Magdalen, Oxford, did not take a degree. It was no different at Cambridge, as Sir Reader Bullard testifies:

I was surprised to find that a very considerable proportion of the undergraduates at Queens' [Cambridge] were drifting through the Pass Degree, which made no great demands on

151

Cambridge, c. 1900

their time and energy. Coming from a world where you flattened your nose against the window of the shop of learning without having the money to go in and make even a modest purchase I felt that the resources of the College were being partly wasted and that some of the Pass Degree men might with advantage be exchanged for some poor students of my acquaintance.

In 1900–1 only 20,000 students received full-time education in the universities. The exclusiveness of the university system aggravated the social rift in the nation, which was symbolized by the antagonism of Town and Gown. There were, of course, progressive elements among the dons, but the tone was set by those who taught the past and mistrusted the future. Sir Llewellyn Woodward, as an undergraduate, read a paper to a society in Corpus, Cambridge, in which he cited facts about the wages of local shop-assistants. The President of his College, without having heard or read the paper, insisted subsequently that he should never again give vent to socialist opinions within the College walls. Sir Lawrence Jones observes of his happy years at Balliol: 'We did not so much as notice that our servants, always about and among us, lived in basements by day and in attics by night; that on their very holidays they wore drab, funereal clothes. But then the Dons did not notice it either.'

Something was beginning to be done, however, for the under-privileged. Ruskin College, founded at Oxford in 1899, offered adult education courses of one year to both men and women, and many trade unionists took advantage of them. The College split in 1909 and the Central Labour College, backed chiefly by the South Wales Miners' Federation and, after 1912, by the National Union of Railwaymen, transferred to London. The Workers' Education Association came into being in 1903 and collaborated with the universities in their extra-mural work.

In general, technical education lagged behind the needs of an age in which the application of science to industry was already of high importance for the country's future. The Technical Instruction Act (1889) had empowered County and County Borough Councils to provide technical education for school-leavers and in 1897 the London County Council set up a Technical Education Board; but after the passage of the Education Act of 1902 local authorities were inclined to concentrate in the first instance on the new field of Secondary Schools. Trade Schools began to be established and a major step forwards was taken in 1907, when the Royal

Applying for books at a free library in Brixton

College of Science, the Royal School of Mines and the City and Guilds of London Institute Engineering College were merged in the Imperial College of Science and Technology, which in the following year became part of the University of London. In the North and Midlands, technical colleges at Birmingham, Leeds and Sheffield received charters as fully-fledged universities; altogether, with the addition of Bristol and Liverpool, five new universities came into existence between 1900 and 1909. England waited over 50 years before again giving birth to so many new institutions of higher learning within so short a space of time.

For the young working-class man who missed even the opportunities offered by evening classes, there remained the public libraries. Books could be borrowed for 2*d.*, but the deposit of 1*s.* and the demand for a recommendation from a resident often proved deterrents. The young student who wanted to get ahead had to compete for a vacant seat or lectern with older men who had long since surrendered every ambition except that of keeping warm and dry. W. H. Davies has drawn this picture of the library as a place of refuge.

> The greatest enemy to the man who has to carry on his body all his wardrobe is rain. . . . To escape from the coming deluge he seeks shelter in the public library, which is the only free shelter available; and there he sits for hours staring at one page, not a word of which he has read or, for that matter, intends to read. If he cannot get a seat, he stands before a paper and performs that almost impossible feat of standing upright fast asleep, so as to deceive the attendants, and respectable people who are waiting a chance to see that very paper. To be able to do this requires many unsuccessful efforts, which fail on account of hard breathing, nodding and stumbling against the paper stand. . . .

Wherever we look, the contrasts of Edwardian life are borne in upon us. As youth and education end, the working-class boy (for in age, if not in experience, he is little more) stands hunched up in the rain before the doors of the public library, which has closed for the day. He is hoping that tomorrow he will find casual labour and will not have to return empty-handed to the dark and dirty back room which he shares with his brothers and small sisters. The Edwardian young man about town, who is dressing for another of those tiresome débutante balls, is wondering whether it will be a warm night, making it advisable to take a spare starched collar with him. The carnation in readiness for his button-hole stands in a glass of water. He rings the bell for his father's valet; it is later than he thought.

Further Reading

Sir J. Mountford, *British Universities*
T. W. Bamford, *Rise of the Public Schools*
G. Greene (ed.), *The Old School*
J. H. Badley, *Memories and Reflections*
Letters of H. E. Luxmoore
P. Coveney, *Image of Childhood*
W. Hillcourt, *Baden-Powell*
P. Green, *Kenneth Grahame*

VIII

The State of Morals and the Rights of Women

Behind every Edwardian man and woman looms the shadow of the Victorian paterfamilias, the author of their being and the authority under whom, in obedience or revolt, they lived out their early lives. There were, of course, many kindly fathers, who tempered their despotism with benevolence; there were also fathers who had abdicated and allowed their thrones to be usurped by wife or mother; but the norm in all classes of society was patriarchal. This father-figure was by no means confined to the middle-class mind. Joseph Ashby, the agricultural reformer, came from a labouring home, of which his daughter writes:

> Their mother would teach them, always by action and sometimes in words, that girls and women find it best to submit to husbands and brothers. Their duty was to feed them well, to run their errands and to bear for them all burdens save physical ones. . . . Of course the main source of the doctrine on women was Father's head! Independence or 'separate action' for women would be 'false, foolish, destructive of women's best and holiest qualities'.

Although brothers might benefit at one remove from father's dominance, it was not just a man's world; it was an old man's world. The bearded figures peer out at us from faded photographs with much of the awesomeness of Jehovah. This is natural enough, since nineteenth-century fathers had their feet

The family, c. 1900

firmly planted in the Old Testament, the Epistles of St Paul and the Protestant Reformation, which had cast out the Whore of Babylon together with Mariolatry and all the soft, effeminate ways of the Mediterranean. Stern fathers based themselves on Pauline doctrine: 'the man is the head of the woman'. Marriage was for the procreation of children and had become a Sacrament of the Church because it was better to marry than to burn. Hell-fire still illuminated sermons in chapel, if not in church, and for Anglo-Saxon Protestantism sexual morality remained the touchstone of all morality. Woman was the source of temptation, as Adam had found. The taboos of society, which were still strong at the turn of the century, were to protect men against themselves and nurture the tender plant of Victorian chivalry towards women of the upper and middle classes.

Fear of the flesh led to swaddling of women in clothes from throat to instep; but natural desire insinuated itself and beneath the dense coverings fashion emphasized the bust and the bustle, until the female figure acquired the shape of an S. Bustles might draw attention to bottoms, but the word must never be spoken. Gwen Raverat records how her sister, on hearing a recitation of Cowper's *Epitaph on a Hare*, inquired, 'What's a rump?' Silence fell on the company, but an aunt afterwards explained, 'I think I ought to tell you that the rump is the back part of an animal, but it is a word you must never, never use!' Human contours were permitted, but not naked flesh. So powerful was this convention in polite society that it extended to the beach and to girls' boarding-schools; older women usually took pains to conceal their nakedness from the candid gaze of children. Sonia Keppel describes the efforts of her nurse to dress without what would have been called 'indecency'.

At one moment I could see the outline of a huge shoulder above the bath; then its emergence again for a tantalizing minute, as she put on her bodice and stertorously pulled up her stays. . . . There followed the camouflage of her petticoat, concealing the pulling on of knickers; more whalebone, more starch, clamping down a vast bosom; the fastening of sharp buckles and a brooch, like the riveting of armour.

Reticence and concealment did not, of course, change anything in human nature; but, as in all ages of chivalry, a man was led to make a firm distinction in his mind between 'a pure woman', who bore his children, and 'a light woman', with whom sex was fun. The distinction resulted in prostitution on a grand scale. James Laver has observed that, 'An epoch which is not an age of promiscuity is necessarily an age of prostitution.' He goes on to point out that, in such an age, 'fashion is dictated by the grande cocotte and tends to favour the older woman.' This analysis, which applies forcibly to the Edwardian period, helps to explain the violence of the reaction of younger women to the society in which they found themselves and the hypocrisy that made it possible. Father's protective attitude towards wife and daughters, however much he might dub himself 'guardian of the vestal flame', was a proprietary one. A woman was a piece of property and a pedestal is often the safest place for property of value. A woman ran a man's home and reared his children. In the upper reaches of society, she received his guests and hired and fired his servants; in the lower strata she cooked his meals and darned his socks. Her liberation would be an infringement of his rights.

'Sacred womanhood' was a fine phrase in the home, but outside it woman was still the instrument of man's pleasure. For
those who took their pleasures seriously, the thriving industry of
prostitution provided whatever was required, including very
young girls, for whom the alternative was sometimes little better
than starvation. The fact that the woman of pleasure was of a
lower class helped to preserve the double standard; the poor
were outside the code of chivalry. Prostitution, like poverty, was
part of the social order; virtue consisted in avoiding scandal and
venereal disease. The latter-day Victorians had been
forced to take cognizance of V.D. because of inroads into the
armed forces and various Acts for Prevention of Contagious
Diseases (as they were euphemistically named) were passed
between 1864 and 1869, which in ports and garrison areas
permitted the police to carry off women for medical examina-
tion on bare suspicion. Women resented this discrimination
against their sex and Mrs Josephine Butler,
with help from male reformers, secured repeal
of the Acts in 1886. The success of this campaign
stimulated the movement for women's suffrage.

The 'spécialité corset'

One of the reformers who did most to throw
open the bedroom windows was Havelock Ellis,
who devoted himself to the new sciences of
eugenics, anthropology and psychology. But in
his enthusiasm for science he avoided the
crude Huxleyan antithesis between science
and religion. For Ellis sex was a manifesta-
tion of the Life Force and his approach,
although backed by careful observation, was
a mystical one. Between 1897 and 1899 Ellis
published the first two volumes of his *Studies
in the Psychology of Sex*, of which four further
volumes were published between 1903 and
1910. He believed that the relations between
the sexes were vitiated by ignorance and
superstition and that impurity flourished behind the veil held up by the prude. The
reaction was predictable; the first two volumes

159

were solemnly burned by Dean Inge, who condemned them as 'unwholesome'. At about the same time a legal attack was mounted against Ellis and his friend Bedborough, who was Secretary of the Legitimation League and legally responsible for the publication of the magazine *Adult*. Bedborough was arrested for 'publishing an obscene libel' and, in response to a discreet promise by the police of lenient treatment if he pleaded guilty, agreed to do so. He was not of the tough material of which martyrs are made.

In the soil that Havelock Ellis and others had cultivated grew the dark flowers of a genius who had begun life in a Nottinghamshire mining village. D. H. Lawrence was no less one of Ellis's spiritual heirs for the fact that he detested psychology and the many philosophies of life struggling to grow where the great oaks of religion had fallen. Lawrence's first novel, *The White Peacock*, was published in 1911. Four years later, when he published *The Rainbow*, the old prudery in public life reasserted itself and a charge of obscenity was brought against him. It was not that the reading public disliked sex as a theme—on the contrary; but they liked it wrapped in a tissue of unreality. The best-seller of 1908 was Dr H. de Vere Stacpole's *The Blue Lagoon*, which depicted two innocents cast away on a tropical island. *Punch* commented, '. . . it is a long time since I read a book more fascinating, more delicately conceived, more healthily nurtured on the fruits of an observation which knows when not to observe.'

One of those who observed too much and too clearly for most Edwardians was Sigmund Freud. A storm broke in 1905, when he published three essays, one of which was devoted to infantile sexuality; its impact was the greater, because it exposed the incompatibility of the dual attitudes adopted by so many parents towards children. In the previous year J. M. Barrie's *Peter Pan* had been produced with resounding success and adults had crowded into the Duke of York's Theatre, assenting vigorously that they believed in fairies and agreeing that children were wayward little darlings, who did not want to grow up. Yet many of the same adults exercised a resolute, if discreet, tyranny in the home and repressed with a stern hand the waywardness that sounded so captivating in the mouths of Peter and Wendy. In the interstices of their mind most fathers and mothers knew well enough about infant masturbation and the sexual manifestations to which Freud gave the designation Oedipus complex; but they had no wish to be reminded of these guilty secrets, long relegated to the subconcious. If one admitted that infants felt cravings which adults regarded as 'unhealthy', what would become of the innocence of childhood? It might be necessary to concede that the only difference between child and adult

Cecilia Loftus, the first Peter Pan

sexuality was that adults were more secretive about it and had succeeded in either repressing the manifestations or directing them into channels which society accepted as legitimate. But such a concession led to a confusion of the labels 'innocent' and 'guilty'; to admit that children and adults were equally innocent or guilty was destructive of authority. It also tended to impair the usefulness of the labels.

If there was no sex education for the young in the Edwardian period, there was certainly conditioning of the minds of girls. Unhappy wives often conveyed to their daughters an obscure sense of resignation before Man the Beast and counselled them, when they too became wives, to tolerate his love-making as best they might. The belief that only 'light women' took pleasure in love-making was widely shared by men. Sir Lawrence Jones in his classic, *An Edwardian Youth*, has related how at an Oxford stag party a doctor was asked whether women enjoyed sexual intercourse. The reply was, 'Speaking as a doctor, I can tell you that nine out of every ten women are indifferent to or actively dislike it; the tenth, who enjoys it, will always be a harlot.' It is pitiable to imagine the predicament of a bridegroom obliged by his upbringing to believe either that his embraces gave his bride no pleasure, or that she was a loose woman. One is reminded of the practice of cliterodectomy by some African tribes, which is intended to discourage brides from finding pleasure in the sex act, and thus from seeking any but a husband's lawful embrace.

Even where parental silence took the place of bad advice, the result was to preserve ignorance rather than innocence. Florence White in *A Fire in the Kitchen* has included recollections of the Rescue Home for Girls in which she worked for a time.

There was one girl, not 15, who looked absolutely dazed; in her arms she held a wizened baby. Its father was her own age. They were children of respectable country folk and they used to walk some distance to school. They had not 'meant to be wicked'; they were only playing without thinking of the consequences. She had been sent away to keep the sad story from her younger sisters.

This was, indeed, the crux of Edwardian morality. To those who could avoid being found out almost everything was permitted. If your vice or indiscretion was exposed, ostracism of some kind was sure to follow. Society was ruled by the twin commandments: Thou shalt not have recourse to Law; Thou shalt not feature in the popular Press. Breaches of these commandments were rarely forgiven. The pretence and the hypocrisy bore most hardly on children. Vyvyan Holland has described the stratagems adopted by his mother's family to prevent his knowing that his father was Oscar Wilde and the strange imaginings created in his mind by the evasions and duplicity that the grown-ups thought proper to employ. He was 18 before any enlightenment was granted to him.

The conspiracy of silence about sex extended to the body and all its functions. In general, girls fared worse than boys. If parents hid the maps and protested that the earth was flat, boys who were prepared to defy them could go out and see for themselves. But for the girls the unexplored territory was peopled with demons, carefully put there—often with the best intentions —not only by fathers, but by mothers, nurses, governesses and school-mistresses as well. In rural homes, especially those of the poor, the facts of life triumphantly asserted themselves; but in middle-class homes all was shrouded in decent obscurity. Young eyes must be averted not only from the improprieties of animals, but even from the nude bodies of boys of six or seven, who might inconveniently be found bathing in the course of a country walk. E. M. Forster in *A Room with a View* describes how his heroine escapes from her chaperone and buys a photograph of Botticelli's 'Birth of Venus': 'Venus, being a pity, spoilt the picture, otherwise so charming, and Miss Bartlett had persuaded her to do without it. (A pity in art of course signified the nude.)'

Gwen Raverat has recorded how, even in broad daylight, a girl was not allowed, without a chaperone, to visit a cathedral in the company of her fiancé. If gentlemen living under the same code were not to be trusted, how much greater the danger from 'rough men'? The same writer remarks, 'The Poor Frightened me very much.' If daylight was dangerous, it was no wonder that the dark was alive with nameless horrors. These fears came in extreme cases to apply to the young girl's own body. She was obliged to ride side-saddle; vigorous exercise was discouraged, for fear of bringing on a haemorrhage, or prolapse. Where maternal exhortation proved insufficient, it was reinforced by medical advice, as if good health and morals consisted in a blameless inertia. After Baden-Powell founded the Boy Scout movement, he was the recipient of the following letter: 'Dear sir, If a girl is not allowed to run, or even to hurry, to swim, ride a bike, or raise her arms above

A domestic scene

'For the development of the muscles'

her head, can she become a Scout? Hoping that you will reply. Sincerely, A Would-be Scout.'

Those who today criticize the young and the decline in their moral standards usually deplore also the decay of family life and parental authority, which is in part ascribed to increased industrial employment of women, stimulated by two world wars. They sometimes forget that the period before 1914, when the pendulum was only beginning to swing in its present direction, was one in which family life seemed to many young people not so much a stabilizing as a sterilizing factor in their lives. It is true that by the end of Victoria's reign the number of these domestic prisons was diminishing and from those which remained the young men were rapidly making their escape. Peter Coveney has described Samuel Butler's *The Way of All Flesh* (1903) as '. . . one of the great solvents of the Victorian family'. A few years later Edmund Gosse performed an even more delicate dissection upon his father in *Father and Son*, in which religious cant is held up to special ridicule. But for daughters the escape route was opening up much more slowly.

For girls, the key to the prison door was education. Without an education more adequate than that which a governess— herself largely uneducated—could provide, the professions were not open to women whose family pride and delicate nurture precluded them from work in industry. Without a profession which their parents would regard as respectable, daughters could not leave home and make themselves independent of father's heavy hand and mother's wish for a daughter's companionship in her declining years. There was a surplus of females in Edwardian England and for middle-class girls, who did not have the benefit of a London season, opportunity did not knock frequently. When it did, the suitor was sometimes subjected to a humiliating cross-examination by parents; he might

164

be shown the door for reasons which might represent parental opinion sincerely held, but which might also cloak the personal convenience of a widower or the selfishness of a mother. Many were the cases in which a suitor's religious views were found to be 'unsound', or his family were condemned as being 'engaged in trade'. The parents of Beatrix Potter 'thought a country solicitor much beneath them'. Their dutiful daughter wrote, 'I see their objections, as we belong to the Bar and the Bench'. She finally married her solicitor in 1913, when she was 47, and the authoress who has given so much joy to children remained childless.

In the second half of the nineteenth century Miss Beale and Miss Buss and other pioneers had provided greater possibilities for girls who wished to improve their minds and could secure parental consent. But a boy's education always took priority and in some homes there was no money to spare for the girls. One such home was that of Sir Lawrence Jones, who himself had the benefit of Eton and Balliol.

A schoolgirl

Equality of opportunity was not yet a political, far less a domestic, slogan. Thousands of other families were economising on the girls to send one bright boy to College. But, in looking back across fifty years, my gratitude for all that was lavished on myself is a little clouded by the reflection that generosity rather than justice went to the shaping of my good fortune. And had I been one of my sisters, I should, I think, have felt the unfairness of it. To have been

Roedean School

wholly untrained for the world would have seemed to me a high price to pay for being kept unspotted by it.

Girls who escaped to boarding-school found themselves in a world of female fantasy, dominated at one remove by the unseen male. Vera Brittain, who went in 1908 to St Monica's, Kingswood, recalls, '. . . almost every girl left school with only two ambitions—to return at the first possible moment to impress her school fellows with the glory of her grown-up toilet, and to be engaged before everybody else'. This apotheosis came after a school career which had probably begun with a 'crush' on the dormitory monitor or games mistress. Both the emotions and the ambitions were an inevitable, if undesired, product of the system. Elizabeth Bowen, who was at Downe House, has written:

> Great friends were not put together and we were not allowed into each other's bedrooms. . . . Assignations for serious or emotional talks connected themselves with the filling of hot-water-bottles and water cans at a tap outside the bathrooms, when one was otherwise ready for bed. Girls of a roving disposition with a talent for intimacy were always about this passage. A radiator opposite this tap was in demand in winter. . . . The radiator was near the headmistress's door, and she would disperse any group she came out and found.

Classics, mathematics and even science had replaced the mid-Victorian curriculum of English grammar and history, drawing, needlework and the 'use of globes', perhaps with French as an extra. It was a great step forward and the teaching was often competent. Unfortunately, the girls' public schools had imported also some of the less useful lumber of Arnold's tradition. Leading schools, such as Roedean and Wycombe Abbey, had adopted school uniforms, the prefect system and house matches. Cricket and Plutarch's *Lives* may, or may not, have been an aid to colonial administrators, but the usefulness of this training for the wife of the Empire-builder was even less evident. The domestic sciences fell into an unmerited and unfeminine contempt. As an educational system it left much to be desired; but at least the public school girls got more learning and more fresh air than their mothers had and were able to reach out into a world, however unreal, beyond the restrictive circle of their own families.

At 18 or 19 school, or the tutelage of a governess, came to an end. For bright girls of middle-class background a new struggle began: to obtain permission to go to a women's college at Oxford, Cambridge or London University, or to embark on training for a profession, as alternatives to living at home. Wells sets the scene in his short novel *The Soul of a Bishop*. The bishop's daughter says to him, '"I would like to go to Newnham or Somerville—and work. I feel—so horribly ignorant. Of all sorts of things. If I were a son I should go."

"You could read here."

"If I were a son, you wouldn't say that."

His reply was vague. "But in this home," he said, "we have a certain atmosphere. . . ."'

A girl from the top of the social scale had a different option; her place in society enabled her to be presented at Court, a proud ordeal which took place in June. She would sit anxiously in her carriage, with three ostrich feathers nodding on her head, and hope her dress was not creasing too badly, whilst the long line of carriages crept towards the Palace and the sightseers did their best to peer in. Once inside, each débutante would be marshalled in order of precedence and the file past would begin. As she came opposite the throne, her name would be called out and she would curtsey three times, as she had been taught to do; more difficult was the retreat backwards to the door, encumbered by her long train. The great marriage

Debutantes being presented to the King and Queen in 1905

Gertrude Bell

market had begun, with a ball every night in one of the great houses of London. The dinners that preceded the ball, apart from that given by the hostess of the evening, had been arranged separately and no débutante could count on arriving at the ball with the group with which she had been dining. She would, of course, have a chaperone with her and the family coachman outside would have as long a vigil as the chaperone inside. Footmen in red livery and knee-breeches would open the doors as the guests streamed in. Then, as later, an adequate supply of young males was a problem and the practice had already begun of passing round from one hostess to another lists of young men who, for the price of their supper, were glad to dance all night. But certain hostesses, such as the Duchess of Northumberland, felt this custom to be beneath their dignity.

These exalted heights were beyond the reach of the vast majority of the female population; but for girls of the lower and lower-middle class opportunities of employment increasingly opened up ways of leaving home, at least during hours of daylight. In 1901 women comprised one-quarter of the total labour force; at the end of the decade 5·4 million women were employed, but only a small proportion were in trade unions. In the factories unions had never welcomed female labour, fearing that expansion of the labour market would depress wages. In 1908, however, the Labour movement finally came out in favour of economic and social equality between the sexes. In certain trades the unions' apprehensions were only too well founded; wages of shop-workers, which were in any case low enough, suffered from the 'pocket-money' wages paid to girls living at home whilst earning a modest supplement to the family exchequer. New work was opening up for women as clerks and telephone operators. In 1901 18 per cent of all clerks were women; by 1911 the percentage had risen to 32. The telephone was a boon to women, as well as to business; by 1900 3,000 female operators were employed and they were soon earning up to 35s. a week. The Post Office opened its first London exchange in 1902, and by 1914 Britain had 775,000 telephones. Although the first automatic exchange had been constructed at Epsom in 1912, this did not as yet endanger employment in a profession to which, from the start, women had established a special claim.

Progress was also being made in other fields; by 1901 there were 212 women doctors and even 140 dentists. By 1910 women could become chartered accountants, though not barristers. Literature, music and the arts, of course, had long been feminine avocations, though some women writers still preferred, as 'George Eliot' had done, to use a masculine pen-name. One of these was 'Laurence Hope', whose 'Indian Love Lyrics' adorned so many occasional-tables and music-stands in Edwardian homes. The walls of these homes might well carry pictures of horses painted by Lucy Kemp-Welch. In the realm of music, Ethel Smyth had already won her reputation; the suffragettes paraded to her 'March of the Women'. Perhaps the most remarkable Edwardian woman—certainly the most versatile—was Gertrude Bell, about whom the rhyme was written:

Mrs Humphrey Ward

From Trebizond to Tripolis
She rolls the Pashas flat
And tells them what to think of this
and what to think of that.

Besides being a linguist, traveller and explorer, she was a naturalist, archaeologist and historian. One thing she was not was a suffragette; indeed during a stay in England in 1908 she became a member of the Women's Anti-Suffrage Committee, in which Mrs Humphrey Ward was also active. The

Committee was later absorbed in the Anti-Suffrage League, in which the leading spirits were those guardians of Empire, Lords Curzon, Cromer and Milner, Joseph Chamberlain and Rudyard Kipling.

In the agitation for women's rights launched in the nineteenth century by Charles Bradlaugh and Annie Besant votes for women had been only one of the planks in their platform; the others were birth control, socialism and liberation from religious orthodoxy. In the last two decades of the century, however, the last three planks were largely abandoned, as Committees of the National Society for Women's Suffrage, which sprang up all over the country, became dominated by the god-fearing middle class and hitched their hopes on to the Liberal Party. After a period of schism among the various suffrage groups, unity was briefly achieved in 1900 with Mrs Garnett Fawcett's National Union of Women's Suffrage Societies, which followed the usual constitutional method of organizing meetings and publicity for the cause. The weakness of this campaign, unkindly dubbed, 'Votes for Ladies', was that it failed to come to terms with the trade unions and, in general, was unable to mobilize the support of women working in industry, except in Lancashire among the mill girls. Mrs Fawcett unwisely opposed a number of measures, designed to make factory work less onerous and dangerous for women, on the ground that such legislation would be discriminatory; she overlooked the argument, stressed by trade unionists, that historically industrial legislation favourable to women had led in time to concessions favouring men also.

One of the women's leaders whose early sympathies with Labour would have fitted her to work with the Independent Labour Party and the unions was Mrs Emmeline Pankhurst, who had become Registrar of Births and Deaths in Manchester after the death of her husband. Unhappily neither Mrs Pankhurst, nor her eldest daughter, Christabel, a law graduate, proved to have the wish or capacity to work with anyone for long. At the outset their eloquence, organizing powers and enthusiasm gave great impetus to the militant splinter group, the Women's Social and Political Union, which they founded in

October 1903. The first acts of
militancy, taking the relatively
mild form of interrupting political meetings, took place in 1905.
In the following year Sylvia
Pankhurst and Annie Kenny,
the mill girl, went to London
with £2 in their pockets to start
work there.

All-out militancy dates from
1908; apart from producing
publicity, it achieved no positive results, unless discrediting
the Liberal Government be
accounted one. If ever a
movement was in need of balanced judgment and collective
leadership, it was the WSPU.
The courage of Mrs Pankhurst
and her and Christabel's capacity to inspire their followers
could not make up for their refusal to accept advice and their
lack of tactical and political in-
sight. If the vote was to be won,

*Mrs Pankhurst and her daughter, Christabel, in
prison uniform, 1908*

a majority in Parliament had to be found; but the political art of
winning friends in high places and applying pressure without
causing offence was never learned and never practised. The
lesson of the campaign against the Contagious Diseases Acts
was forgotten. In 1906, when a Liberal landslide took place, the
WSPU concentrated its attack on the Liberal candidate in
North West Manchester, Winston Churchill, who at that time
had shown no antipathy to the cause. In 1907 the WSPU
severed its connection with the ILP which was in the main
friendly; in 1911 it actually showed itself hostile to unions,
which were on strike, and in 1912 it directed its attacks indis-
criminately against all Labour and Irish MPs, as well as
against its usual victims, the Liberals. By 1913 Christabel, who

173

had taken refuge in Paris, seems to have become unbalanced. She published a book, *The Great Scourge*, in which it was alleged that 75–80 per cent of all men suffered from venereal disease. It was as if she and her mother were determined to alienate everyone on whom the success of their cause depended. They even excommunicated Sylvia Pankhurst, who was working in the East End of London in the belief that it was there that the sufferings of the unenfranchized working woman were most in evidence. The outbreak of war rescued the WSPU from the dead end into which the fanaticism and irrationality of Christabel and her mother had driven it.

To criticize the WSPU does not, of course, imply any approval of the handling of militancy by Asquith's successive governments, which failed to pursue a consistent or conciliatory policy. The Cat and Mouse Act reflected no credit on Parliament and administrative measures were also taken which were both inhuman and calculated to increase sympathy for the women. Conspicuous among these were forcible feeding, both oral and rectal, of hunger-strikers and the willingness of police to allow gangs of hooligans to break up women's meetings with obscene violence. Mary Richardson in her book, *Laugh a Defiance* (the title is taken from the 'March of the Women') recalls one such occasion. 'I shall always remember the hateful, weasel face of one man in the mob. Like his fellows, he wore a lock of a woman's hair in the buttonhole of his

Miss Ogston hitting stewards at the Albert Hall during a speech by Lloyd George on 'Woman's Suffrage' in 1908

lapel—they wore our hair like trophies in their coats in those days.' An ignoble attempt was made to have Miss Richardson certified in Holloway Gaol as a lunatic, despite her claim to have converted the Bishop of London to the suffragette cause.

Parliament had been dilatory; up to 1905 18 major debates had taken place without result in the preceding 38 years. None the less, violence breeds violence and it was a strange decision to discard the indirect means by which a woman usually gains her point and attack head on with weapons more suited to a man. Mary Richardson slashed a Velazquez Venus in the National Gallery; Emily Davison threw herself in front of a racehorse; others committed arson and tore the clothes off Cabinet Ministers. Much was wrong with society and the status of women within it; but the deepest ills lay outside the reach of legislators. To the extent that these have since been remedied, the change has been due to a long process of education and adjustment and it would be difficult to demonstrate that voting rights have proved to be a decisive factor. The militant movement was to this extent both irrational and irrelevant; it can only be explained as a passionate upsurge of pent-up frustration. The sufferings of millions of oppressed governesses, down-trodden wives and unmarriagable daughters had at last found a voice, even if it was a voice which the overwhelming majority of them in their conscious minds disowned.

One of those who became exasperated with the militants was H. G. Wells, who had his own ideas about how women could become free. He wrote, 'If women wanted to be free, the first thing was surely for them to have complete control of their persons, and how could this happen unless Free Love and Neo-Malthusianism (i.e. birth control) replaced directed and obligatory love and involuntary child-bearing. . . .' In his impatience with the structure of society and the religious sanctions that helped to keep it in place he was harking back to the earlier tradition of Annie Besant and Bradlaugh; but Wells went further by assailing the institution of marriage. He was not first in the field; Grant Allen's *The Woman Who Did* had already depicted a woman who broke social convention by bearing an illegitimate child. Grant Allen's book infuriated

175

Wells, but for a reason different from that which excited most of his contemporaries; he was sure he could have done it better; *The Woman Who Did*, in his view, 'was really a sentimental novelette'. Wells knew what he was talking about. His experience of living before marriage with his second wife, Catherine Robbins, had familiarized him with the weight of the taboos in all classes of society. He wrote later of the marriage, 'The behaviour of the servants of that period and the landladies and next-door neighbours forced that on us anyhow. Directly the unsoundness of our position appeared, servants became impertinent and neighbours rude and strange.'

Public outcry resulted from the publication in 1905 of *A Modern Utopia*, in which Wells praised free love, whilst making it clear that this concession was for the élite, who were found to be fitted for it. Wells subsequently wrote of the book, that it 'was popular among the young of our universities. . . . It played a considerable part in the general movement of release from the rigid technical chastity of women. . . .' In *Socialism and the Family* Wells repudiated what he described as 'private ownership of women and children'. He advocated that 'The state will pay for children born legitimately in the marriage it will sanction. A woman with healthy and successful offspring will draw for each one of them a wage from the state.' If he were living in the Welfare State, Wells might perhaps claim that the introduction of Family Allowances had in a manner fulfilled his hopes without any obligation on the married couple to obtain State approval or to demonstrate that their offspring were 'healthy and successful'. In his own day, however, Wells was far in advance of his fellow socialists, to whom he was increasingly becoming an embarrassment. In 1908 the Conservative, Joynson-Hicks, whose views on sex were later to become a byword for obscurantism, declared in an election campaign that socialism threatened the sacred rights of the family and would reduce women to concubinage. The Labour Party lost no time in repudiating Wells's rejection of conventional marriage.

Wells's views were always more persuasive when expressed in fiction and none of his polemical writings were as cogent as *Ann Veronica*, which appeared in 1909. His gay, courageous

176

Elinor Glyn reclining—on some cushions

heroine was condemned by spokesmen of the Church and dubbed a whore by the *Spectator*, which found the book 'capable of poisoning the minds of those who read it'. This line of argument is still fashionable in book-banning quarters today. Wells himself summed up the nature of the offence against conventional morality: 'The particular offence was that Ann Veronica was a virgin who fell in love and showed it, instead of waiting, as all popular heroines had hitherto done, for someone to make love to her. It was held to be an unspeakable offence that an adolescent female should be sex-conscious before the thing was forced upon her attention.'

Wells was a reformer and inured to suffering vexation for his beliefs. Not so Elinor Glyn, whose career as a novelist began with a laudable desire to pay off some of her husband's debts. *The Vicissitudes of Evangeline* (1906) was regarded as a little *risqué*, but nothing worse. Evangeline, lying in bed in a night-gown with 'short sleeves ruffled with Valenciennes . . . fine linen cambric nicely embroidered,' and looking very becoming, is thus rebuked: 'Becoming! But no nice woman wants things to look becoming in bed!' *Three Weeks*, which appeared in the following year, was more daring, as well as more exotic. The fictional Paul Verdrayne, having escaped to Lucerne from a conventional English rural fiancée, is seduced on a tiger skin by a Balkan Queen, travelling incognito. She was 'garbed in some strange clinging garment of heavy purple crepe . . . between her lips was a rose not redder than they—an almost scarlet rose'. Her technique strikes one, even today, as being of some interest. 'She purred as a tiger might have done, while undulating like a snake.' She was clearly right to travel incognito and no doubt richly deserved to conceive the son who eventually succeeded to the throne of the Balkan King, her impotent husband.

It was the episode of seduction that gave rise to the rhyme:

> *Would you like to sin*
> *With Elinor Glyn*
> *On a tiger skin?*
> *Or would you prefer*
> *To err with her*
> *On some other fur?*

But *The Daily Telegraph* took it more seriously: 'The record of these erotic passions . . . only avoids by a hair-breadth the accusation of growing positively squalid. . . .' Elinor Glyn was charged with 'lack of delicacy and refinement'. The Headmaster of Eton forbade his boys to read the book and, when a dramatic version was made, the Lord Chamberlain would not allow it to be staged. It was not clear whether he thought the play obscene or whether, as some alleged, the Foreign Office considered it likely to give offence in the Balkans. Needless to add that the attitude of the arbiters of morals ensured the success of the book and its authoress. A room at the Cavendish Hotel was named after her and in nine years two million copies of the book were sold.

Novelists, reformers, suffragists, all combined to keep the relationship between the sexes in the forefront of public interest. Parliament, though unwilling to grant the franchise, felt obliged to make some move. In 1909 it set up a Royal Commission on Divorce and Matrimonial Causes, under the Chairmanship of Lord Gorell, lately President of the Divorce and Admiralty Division of the High Court, to inquire into the legal disabilities under which married women laboured. Of the 14 members originally nominated, two were women—much to the disapproval of Edward, who believed matrimonial causes lay

In the Divorce Court

outside a woman's competence. In summoning witnesses the Commission showed even less generosity towards the weaker sex; only 24 of the 246 witnesses were women. The law, as it stood, discriminated not only between men and women, but also, in practice, between rich and poor. Whilst a man could be granted divorce solely on the ground of his wife's adultery, a woman was required to prove against her husband some additional offence, such as desertion (a minimum of two years), cruelty, bigamy, incest or sodomy. Cases could only be heard at a single Court in London and it was estimated that even an undefended suit cost from £50 to £60; a defended case might cost anything up to £500. Of 908 cases that came before the Court in 1910 the males involved in 689 of them were found to have given the following list of occupations: trade (344); professional employment (267); gentlemen, esquires, etc. (78). It was clear that few poor men could afford divorce and that a poor woman without a profession, who had to depend on a husband's largesse in order to divorce him, had virtually no prospect of severing the marriage tie. The Commission, by majority, found that lack of means to pay for divorce forced both men and women into illicit unions. Among those in a

179

position to bring suit, however, the disproportion between men and women was not as great as might have been expected. A yearly average of 638 decrees *nisi* was granted between 1906 and 1910, of which an average of 289 resulted from petitions by wives.

The Commission, which reported in 1912, recommended, 'in the interests of morality . . . and in the general interests of society and the State', that both forms of discrimination should be remedied by establishing equality of the sexes before the law and introducing local jurisdiction, where poor persons' procedure could be applied. The main disagreement within the Commission concerned grounds for divorce. Apart from changing the law in favour of women petitioners, no alteration of existing grounds was proposed; but the Commission, by majority, recommended that Courts exercise discretion, as is done to this day, in favour of a guilty party. Previously it had been established by precedent that cross-charges of adultery, admitted or proved on both sides, had the effect of prolonging the marriage. New grounds for divorce, such as 'unconquerable aversion' and 'mutual consent', were dismissed each in one short paragraph as inadequate. Collusive effort by both parties to terminate a marriage continued to inhibit this result.

A minority report signed by Cosmo Lang, then Archbishop of York, together with a Baronet and a Knight, opposed any extension of divorce facilities, believing that the institution of the family was already threatened by 'a) the assertion of individual liberty; and b) the claims of logical Socialism'. The minority did not deal with the supposed benefits conferred by the family, as an institution, in a home maintained only by the poverty of a couple unable to meet the cost of divorce, or a home in which, because of lack of divorce facilities, a couple were unable to marry and legitimize their children. The minority made much of the evidence of three witnesses of the Mothers' Union (Church of England), which had organized a petition against cheapening or extending divorce, in the belief that to do so would 'injure the home life of the country'. The Archbishop's report contains an allusion to the declining birth rate, and—obliquely—to the practice of contraception, by pointing out that failure 'to accept the discipline of marriage is shown in the growing reluctance to accept its natural consequence, the production and rearing of children'.

It is a revealing commentary on the plight of an established Church—identified as it must be with the established order—that the Church of England was unable to adopt a positive stance towards the two great reforming movements of the Edwardian period, namely the liberation of women and the demand for social justice for the lowest paid workers, male and female. Although many Christians, as individuals, identified themselves with these causes, the Church, as an institution, denied the compassion of its creed and stood apart. The estrangement between Church and people, of which we are sadly conscious today, derives partly from this attitude and partly from the popular assumption of an antagonism between religion and science, which the Church in Victorian times had itself done much to promote. The great prelates of the Church manned the dikes and watched the flood waters of change roll in; when the water-level fell, it was seen that there remained behind a chasm between traditional religion and public morals, which it has proved impossible to bridge.

Further Reading

G. Raverat, *Period Piece*
A. C. Marshall, *Havelock Ellis*
Lamb and Pickthorn, *Locked-up Daughters*
M. Ramelson, *Petticoat Rebellion*
F. White, *A Fire in the Kitchen*
H. Mitchell, *The Hard Way Up*
A. Glyn, *Elinor Glyn*
P. Fryer, *The Birth Controllers*

IX

The Press, Entertainment and Sport

The Late Victorian and Early Edwardian periods saw the foundations laid of the mass media, as we know them today. This was a development of incalculable importance, though its impact did not become apparent before the First World War. Men's minds grew more malleable; the traditional British eccentric, who had been found at both ends of the social scale, began to disappear and the conformist took his place. More men became more widely informed about the world around them; but their information was often of a more superficial kind than that available a century earlier to the small ruling minority. After the First World War, which gave rise to an explosion of political propaganda, operated by governments, those on the receiving end grew a little more wary; but there can be no doubt about the effect of the mass media in conditioning minds to accept generalized political and social attitudes, even if resistance is shown on specific issues.

These developments, however, were implicit, rather than explicit, in the years under survey in these pages. The exploitation of sound waves in wireless telegraphy seemed an unmixed boon when on New Year's Day 1903 King Edward and President Theodore Roosevelt exchanged greetings by Morse code across the Atlantic. Similarly, nothing but approving interest was expressed in 1896, when the Photographer Royal made a film at Windsor of the Tsar and Tsarina planting a tree, or when the first public performance of a moving picture took place in the same year at the Regent Street Polytechnic. Nobody foresaw that, in time, light waves would carry pictures and that light and sound waves would lend themselves to all forms of communication, both for education and entertainment.

Another event occurred in 1896, which, although less obviously part of the technological revolution, had a greater influence on the lives of Edwardians: the publication of Alfred Harmsworth's *Daily Mail*. Whilst printing was as old as Caxton, Harmsworth brought to it both new ideas and new methods. He seized eagerly upon linotype and photographic reproduction and installed folding machines, which spared the housemaid the labour of ironing her master's morning paper. Wireless telegraphy brought news on to the breakfast-table whilst servants of state in War and Foreign Office were still anxiously awaiting 'official confirmation'. For all these services *Daily Mail* readers paid no more than one halfpenny.

The nineteenth century had seen the introduction of primary education for all; but the newspapers, before Alfred Harmsworth and Arthur Pearson swung into the ascendant, had continued to be produced primarily for the well-educated man of leisure, who unfolded in his club—though not without some difficulty—the large sheets of *The Times*, filled with dense, unbroken columns of print. After important debates, speeches in Parliament were often printed in full; it was a convenience to the ruling class, but a sigh of relief went up in the City and in many suburban and provincial homes, when Harmsworth began printing 'The Busy Man's Paper'. His *Daily Mail* and Pearson's *Daily Express*, which followed in 1900, were family newspapers, dealing with home and foreign news in a concise way and breaking up long columns with sub-headings. Photographs reflected reality better than the old-fashioned line drawings; a column of social gossip catered for those preferring the flight from reality. There were household hints and the fancies of fashion on the women's page and even a children's corner. The *Daily Mail* City page was not a dreary summary of current prospectuses, but aimed to give both guidance and protection to the investor. It was no wonder that at the turn of the century one million copies of the *Mail* were selling daily.

Northcliffe

In 1899 both the *Mail* and the *Daily Telegraph* had tried to move into the field of the Sunday paper, where a gap had opened between the extremes of the sober, but unprofitable, *Observer* and the less sober and more profitable *News of the World*. Sabbatarian opinion, which was powerful, approved grudgingly of the *Observer*, which sold for a respectable 2*d*., but raised hands in horror at the *News of the World*'s coverage of crime and divorce. The headlines: 'Ghastly Story of the Fate of a Little Girl', or 'Vicar's Long Intrigue with Nurse', were illuminated with sketches made by reporters within Court precincts. Although Harmsworth's punctiliousness would have kept him clear of the sordid and salacious, Puritan opinion was too strong, and both new Sunday papers gave up after a few weeks. Harmsworth entered the field two years later, however, by buying the *Weekly Dispatch* (later *Sunday Dispatch*).

In 1903 Harmsworth tried out another innovation: the *Daily Mirror* was conceived as a newspaper for women and largely produced by women. The venture failed and, after he had lost £100,000, he transformed it into the first tabloid paper. The *Daily Graphic* had already been in existence for some years, but it could not match the range and quality of the *Mirror*'s photographic reproduction. No story in the *Mirror* exceeded 250 words and, with a staff including such men as Hannen Swaffer, it soon established a reputation for lively journalism and was selling 400,000 a day. It liked to stir up readers to write to the editor on such topics as whether Mr Balfour should play golf on Sunday, or whether it was legitimate for a bachelor girl to have a mild flirtation on her summer holiday. Photographs of engaged girls from high society were a speciality; but Harmsworth papers were allowed no 'cheesecake'. In the summer of 1905 one of the *Mirror*'s stunts was to follow a fair Australian swimmer, Miss Kellerman, round the South Coast resorts; but she was either photographed fully clad or, if she was in the water, only her head was above the surface.

These new developments were, up to a point, admirable. Newspapers stimulated, and in some measure satisfied, readers' curiosity about the lives of their fellow men and the world shared in common by all. Harmsworth and Pearson and those who followed them knit together the inhabitants of these islands as surely as did the railways and motor buses. Men became familiar with the face of the Prime Minister, even if they were not much clearer about his policies. Those who were not politically minded could learn from the *Mail* how to make a house telephone, or a rabbit hutch, or how to grow better roses. Yet Harmsworth's biographers, Reginald Pound and Geoffrey Harmsworth, do not exaggerate when they state: 'Harmsworth journalism changed the relationship of press and public. It destroyed the old, enlightened view that reason would prevail.' The popular Press could not be primarily rational and continue faithfully to reflect the mass mind, which wished to be amused, titillated and, occasionally, 'purged with pity and terror'.

'News', as Alfred Harmsworth defined it, 'is anything out of the ordinary'. The definition is a sound one, in terms of selling newspapers, but it ignores the fact that, for most people most of the time, it is the ordinary that predominates. Harmsworth brought the outside world closer to his readers—the vast majority of them saw no other reflection of it—but it was a distorted world. Harmsworth, at least in the early years of his success, was scrupulous about facts; but the picture of the world presented by his papers was out of focus and over-animated. It moved as people moved in primitive films—with staccato gestures and at impossible speeds. Harmsworth's motto was: 'Explain, Simplify, Clarify'. Even a highly skilled and conscientious journalist, however, can only observe these imperatives if he has a point of view and almost unlimited space. The point of view, even if the proprietor has no prejudices of his own, is imposed by the need to excite and retain interest and to find a selective principle in the face of the volume of available material.

Arthur Pearson

The popular Press, whatever its virtues, showed itself less and less able, or willing, to draw for its readers a distinction between news and views.

Harmsworth was certainly not a proprietor without prejudices; his belief in the family, the capitalist system and the Empire was deep and passionate. Above all, he believed in Harmsworth and the right of a rich and successful man to exert a political influence proportionate to his commercial power. At a comparatively early stage of his career, Lord Esher, meeting him for the first time, summed him up as 'full of aspirations for power'. By 1905, when Harmsworth was ennobled as Lord Northcliffe, he had become increasingly dissatisfied by what seemed to him to be the relative lack of influence upon events exerted by his mass sales. In an attempt to rectify matters, he purchased the *Observer*, which at that date sold only 4,000 copies each Sunday. Three years later he had pushed up sales to 30,000 and installed James Garvin, a Liverpool-Irish journalist and lapsed Catholic, as editor. There was no leader-writer in political journalism better informed than Garvin and he shared Northcliffe's Germanophobia and devotion to Imperialism.

Northcliffe was still unsatisfied. He proceeded to buy *The Times*, which was in financial difficulties, for £320,000. Its circulation had fallen to 38,000 a day, but its reputation as twoway channel between 'top people' and Government had survived. Northcliffe did not secure it without a struggle, in which a judicious leak at the expense of his rival, Arthur Pearson, played its part. Pearson, who gave generously to charity, was a tycoon of a different type. He was an Old Wykehamist and son of a Church of England clergyman; yet he was described by Joseph Chamberlain as 'the greatest hustler I have ever known'.

186

He shared Chamberlain's Imperialism and on Empire Day, 1908 began to publish the *Standard of Empire*, which was intended to concentrate on Empire news and even on Empire advertising. But Pearson was primarily a businessman, lacking Northcliffe's driving political ambition. It was Northcliffe who set the unhappy pattern of newspaper proprietors seeking to use their product to manipulate men's minds for political ends. He was followed along this road by a Canadian businessman, who in the last years before the First World War was coming to the fore in the City and House of Commons. His name was Max Aitken and by 1911 he had a large stake in Pearson's *Daily Express*. Pearson was going blind and dropping out of the race.

Northcliffe aspired not only to control public opinion, but to influence Government directly. His ownership of *The Times* seemed likely to be an effective lever. J. A. Spender, Editor of the Liberal *Westminster Gazette*, has written, 'At that time there was no regular means of communication between the Government and the Press. It was understood and thought proper that Ministers should communicate with *The Times*, but all communications with other papers had to be disguised and were thought to be slightly improper.' After 1908 exacerbation of party politics and Northcliffe's vigorous Conservatism made Liberal Ministers more reluctant to feed information into this channel. But there was one issue on which inside information was readily forthcoming; Admiral Sir John Fisher made it his business to see that not only the Opposition leader, Balfour, but also Garvin was supplied with the ammunition necessary to keep up pressure on the Government to adopt a larger naval building programme than was

Max Aitken (later Lord Beaverbrook) in 1905

Mrs Pat Campbell in a scene from Sophocles' Electra, 1908

acceptable to radicals, both inside and outside the Cabinet, who wanted the money to go into the new social services. This naval campaign fitted perfectly with Northcliffe's self-imposed mission, 'to warn the British people of the coming German peril'. Ever since the Boer War he had preached consistently and with growing violence the inevitability of war with Germany. His visits to that country reinforced his prejudice; on one such visit he wrote, 'Every one of the new factory chimneys here is a gun pointed at England.' In 1913, when Northcliffe was urging the British Government to build dirigibles, *Daily Mail* readers started seeing phantom Zeppelins in the night sky over Yorkshire. It was in these years that the British and German Press began trading insults across the North Sea, a habit which unhappily still survives. To ascribe to Northcliffe a major share of responsibility for the outbreak of the First World War would be to share his exaggerated egotism; but it is interesting to speculate what influence in the direction of peace might have been exerted if the political direction of Northcliffe's papers had been entrusted to Norman Angell, one-time manager of the Continental *Daily Mail*. Angell published in 1909 his book *The Great Illusion*, in which he convincingly exposed the moral and economic fallacies underlying the promotion of patriotic causes tending towards war.

Soon after Northcliffe took over *The Times*, he complained of the paucity of its coverage of theatre and sport. It was indeed true that pleasure-loving Edwardians rated stage and sport only a little below the delights of the bed and the table. By 'the stage' must be understood the very different worlds inhabited by such celebrities as Mrs Patrick Campbell, Marie Lloyd, Isadora Duncan, Pavlova and Melba; but it is to the legitimate theatre and the music-hall that we shall address ourselves, since these reflected social interests on the largest scale.

The world of the theatre was animated and prosperous in Edwardian days and it may occasion surprise that it came under such severe criticism. One of the reasons for this can be expressed simply by citing the name of the leading critic: George Bernard Shaw. Whatever plays had been offered by the actor-managers of the day, Shaw would have found something corruscating to say about them, because to do so was in his nature and lay on his path to fame. But Shaw's criticism had serious basis; it was rooted in his attitude as a moralist. He believed that the theatre should instruct and improve and he had no sympathy with those who regarded it solely as a medium of entertainment and profit. 'Modern civilisation,' he affirmed, 'is rapidly multiplying the class to which the theatre is both school and church.'

To suggest that the theatre was in decline at the turn of the century would be to do less than justice to its main pillars, Arthur Wing Pinero and Henry Arthur Jones. Pinero was even making efforts to come to terms with Ibsen, and Max Beerbohm

Ellen Terry in a scene from Shaw's Captain Brassbound's Conversion, *1906*

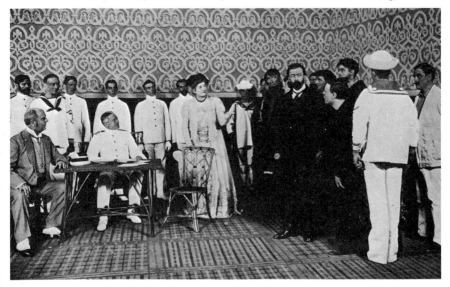

Henry Irving

slyly alluded to Pinero's 'latest assortment of Spring Problems (Scandinavian Gents' own materials made up. West End style and fit guaranteed)'. It was indeed Ibsen who was to blame for disturbing the equanimity of West End actor-managers: the Theatre of Ideas was his temple and William Archer was his prophet. To Shaw, as to Archer, it seemed that 'the Woman with a Past' of the sophisticated London stage did not bear comparison, as a human being and subject of observation, with Hedda Gabler and other sombre and emancipated heroines from Scandinavia. Drawing-room comedies, in which potentially tragic situations were handled with a light touch and led to a happy ending, seemed to the *avant-garde* critics to represent an alienation from reality. So, too, did the lavish and often melodramatic spectacles offered by Sir Henry Irving at the Lyceum. Even when Irving performed Shakespeare's plays, Shaw was not appeased, describing them as 'gorgeous stage ritualism superimposed on ruthless mutilations of his [Shakespeare's] text'.

It must be said in favour of conventionally minded playwrights and managers that they suffered heavily under the prevailing censorship. As Richard Findlater, the latest historian of censorship, has pointed out, 'Between 1895 and 1909, out of some 8,000 plays submitted to the Chamberlain only 30 were banned. But these included works by some of the leading writers of the age.' Among the victims were Ibsen, Tolstoy, Maeterlinck, D'Annunzio and Gerhardt Hauptmann; those nearer home included Oscar Wilde, Granville Barker, Laurence Housman and, of course, Shaw himself. The damage was not confined to plays sent in for censorship; many were unborn because of advice received from experienced managers, whose livelihood depended on divining the whims of the examiner before capital was invested. The examiner's main criterion was simple: if the topic was a traditional one, treated in a traditional way, it was acceptable. For preference, it should be a trivial subject, frivolously treated. When in 1909 the agitation of playwrights obliged Parliament to set up a Joint Select Committee on Censorship, Sir Herbert Tree said, in evidence, of a rejected play, 'I was told that it would be unacceptable—the subject was adultery—but if it could be made more comic, it would pass.' The fact that a subject was dealt with in a serious spirit did not give it immunity; it condemned it. The censor did not stand alone. In 1907 *The Times* wrote of Granville Barker's *Waste*, 'The subject matter of *Waste*, together with the sincere realism with which it is treated, makes it in our judgment wholly unfit for performance, under ordinary conditions, before a miscellaneous public of various ages, moods and standards of intelligence.' The disservice rendered to serious drama by this attitude needs no emphasis.

Beerbohm Tree as Cardinal Wolsey

Sir Henry Irving was the Grand Old Man of the stage. Neville Cardus recalls Irving's farewell appearance at the Manchester Theatre Royal, before his departure on an American tour. 'At the end of the performance he came before the curtain and

A design by Gordon Craig for Act 1 of Hamlet, *1903*

spoke to us in his sepulchral voice, bidding us "Good-bye". And the audience rose as one man and sang "God be with you till we meet again."' In October 1905 at Bradford, after a performance of Tennyson's *Becket,* he said good-bye for the last time. The grand manner was carried on at His Majesty's by Tree. After seeing an adaptation of *Edwin Drood* in 1908, the *Daily Mail*'s critic described it as 'a gorgeous melodramatic production of opium thrills and agonies—the whole thing being a crowning example of Mr Tree's "heroic" stage management'. Ellen Terry's admiration for Irving did not falter but—with a woman's catholicity—she helped to finance productions devised by her son, Gordon Craig, who held the 'encumbered realistic' stage in abhorrence. He aspired, as Sir John Gielgud has put it, to 'a theatre of sound and mood and light, of music, masks, movement, dance and pantomine . . .'. His touch was too delicate for Edwardian England and little was seen of him in London after his departure to Berlin in 1904.

Shaw's quarrel with the commercial theatre, in which he was joined by Galsworthy, was not so much that it aimed to make money, but that it did so in an unimaginative and illogical way. The manager, according to Shaw, pandered to the gallery, who loved sentimental romance, but paid only 1*s.* for their seats, when he should have directed his appeal to the stalls, who paid 10*s.* 6*d.* Shaw maintained that, in the stalls, the rich 'demand edification, and will not pay for anything else in that

arena. Consequently the box-office will never become an
English influence until the theatre turns from the drama of
romance and sensuality to the drama of edification.' It cannot
be said that the Independent and the New Century Theatres,
where the New Drama was performed, achieved a success that
vindicated Shaw's flattery of the cultured rich. But in Manchester, which took its culture seriously, it was another story.
The heroine of the Manchester School was Miss Horniman,
who at the Gaiety Theatre gave encouragement to young
dramatists like Stanley Houghton, author of *Hindle Wakes*.
Neville Cardus recaptures the mood:

> Miss Horniman, a delightful spinster who openly smoked
> cigarettes in the lounge of the Midland Hotel, gave me and

Camille Clifford, the original Gibson Girl   *Lily Elsie in* The Merry Widow, *1907*

countless other young men of Manchester our first contact with the 'play of ideas', as we called it, bless us. And the *Manchester Guardian* sniffed at the 'commercial theatre'. . . . An outbreak of the Manchester School of Drama set in—Houghton, Brighouse and Monkhouse. The action of their plays usually began in the Eccles New Road; the son and heir of old Seth Northcote—Manchester Home Trade—had got Jessie, one of the maids, with child.

It is a far cry from the Manchester Gaiety to George Edwardes's Gaiety in London, where so many young peers of the realm lost their hearts and, in their parents' eyes, debased their coronets. Though dowagers would still say of a younger and prettier woman, 'Anyone would take her for an actress!', the status of the stage was rising and the grace and wit of Gaiety girls had something to do with it; Gladys Cooper was briefly a Gaiety girl. The gay musical was highly popular entertainment; Edwardes's *The Country Girl* ran from January 1902 to January 1904. At the Savoy the D'Oyly Carte held high the flag of Gilbert and Sullivan. Good tunes, with the lilt of Vienna, came to London a few years later with *The Merry Widow*.

Musical comedy and operetta, with some pretence of plot, fall midway between the legitimate theatre and the music-hall, though the latter entertainment owed its origin to no playwright or librettist. The music-hall in its earliest years was no more than a device to keep the drinking clientele quietly in their seats whilst their glasses were refilled. To this origin the halls were indebted for the agreeable informality which pervaded them and their exemption from the attentions of the censor. Prices were low, because the sale of liquor helped to pay the rent; the artistes' fees were low, because

Dan Leno

194

the multitude of Halls enabled them to perform at several in one night, with a hansom cab waiting at the stage-door. Variety theatres and music-halls in their hundreds spread, as cinemas were to do later, throughout the London suburbs. The Empire chain included Hackney, Holloway, New Cross, Stratford, Shepherd's Bush and Islington. The Pavilion and Tivoli syndicates were also extensive. Here one might see Cinquevalli juggling, or Houdini escaping from handcuffs; Dan Leno would be a down-trodden waiter or henpecked husband, and George Robey would do a female impersonation ('I'm a lone, lonely lady and I've not a friend on earth, Without a set of teeth to call my own . . .'). Will Fyffe 'Belonged to Glasgow';

George Robey

Nellie Wallace was 'Down by the River Side' and Albert Chevalier 'Knocked 'em in the Old Kent Road'. And, if one was lucky, the inimitable Marie Lloyd would sing in that 'gruffy' voice 'Follow the Van' or perhaps 'The Smartest Girl in Town'.

Mabel's got a houseboat on the Thames, River Thames!
Mabel wears the most expensive gems, lovely gems!
A flat (you would adore it!)
And nothing to pay for it,
A thing that smart society condemns!

At 'at homes' she does Tableaux Vivants, Oh! Vivants!
Fellows come and gather round in throngs, perfect throngs!
They say, 'By Jove, it's fine'
And admire her form divine;
They can't do better on the Continong.

195

The Edwardians, who seemed to be witnessing the Halls in their heyday, were also seeing the beginning of the end. Capital was moving in and transforming them into larger Palaces of Variety, where the intimate touch was lost. New proprietors, like Oswald Stoll, were going in for family entertainment and the tone was rising. At Christmas some of the shining lights of the Halls went into pantomine. Beside the sea the Pierrots were putting on shows fit for all age groups, at which new reputations were made. Tom Walls began his career on the

Marie Lloyd, the epitome of cheerful vulgarity

pier at Brighton, earning £2 5s. a week. The new entertainers were much loved, but they lacked the earthiness of the older shows. Moreover, the Halls had in some real way mirrored and transfigured the lives of the poor, with their eternal optimism about an inheritance and their eternal pessimism about the hard facts of married life once the honeymoon was over.

Stars of the Halls believed their enemy was the phonograph; but, in fact, the foe lurked at the end of the programme in the form of the new-fangled Bioscope. In bleak cities, where the public house offered almost the only alternative to the congested home, the cinema, at prices from 3d. to 1s. 6d., increasingly came to provide shelter from the cold and a flight into a world in which there were fewer limitations to human potentiality. By 1914 London music-halls were more and more being converted to use as cinemas and every large town in Britain boasted at least one Bijou, Gem, Pallasimo or Picturedrome. The cinema was at once recognized by harassed parents as a good place for a child on a wet day. One Saturday afternoon in mid-winter 1908 moving pictures were due to be shown to children in a hall in Barnsley; 433 pennies had already been taken at the door, when a panic occurred on the stairs leading to the gallery. After it had subsided, 16 children aged between four and nine were found crushed to death in a mass, according to one witness, about five feet high. In the following year the licensing of cinemas was made a responsibility of local authorities.

Early audiences showed their taste for violence; a successful film dealt with the depredations and hanging of a well-known criminal, Charlie Peace. Animated cartoons also date from this period. Sentiment was well served in 1905 by a one-reeler, *Rescued by Rover*, which depicted the faithful hound saving baby's life. In 1907 the scenario writers turned their attention to *Black Beauty*. The situations in which the speechless performers found themselves were often as absurd as their gestures; but it was not a reflection of real life that the audience was seeking. The alternate rumble and tinkle of the piano, shrouded in darkness below the screen, fed the illusion and heightened tension.

Edwardians who queued for the cinema queued also to cheer their sporting heroes on a Saturday afternoon; Britain was well on the way to becoming a nation of non-participating sportsmen. Association Football dominated the industrial North and Midlands and drew the largest crowds; on an average Saturday in January 1908, 32 Cup-Ties were watched in all by 450,000 people. Later in the same year, when Wolverhampton Wanderers (then in the Second Division)

A scene from Rescued by Rover

defeated Newcastle United (First Division) by 3 goals to 1 in the Final, nearly 75,000 fans saw the game. Soccer was already sufficiently commercialized for players to be bought and sold for substantial fees; at the end of the 1904–5 season Middlesbrough transferred a player to Sunderland for £1,000.

Spectators also crowded in to the cricket grounds of the 16 first-class counties. Neville Cardus remembers how it felt to be a young enthusiast on 26 June 1902:

The match between Chelsea and Sheffield Wednesday, 1908

On this radiant day I set forth; my hero J. T. Tyldesley at the close of play on the previous evening had finished 36 not out. I had to walk six miles, for somehow I took a wrong turning, and found myself on the other side of the canal and I could not get over; so I ran on and on, terrified at the thought that Tyldesley was making brilliant strokes and I was not there. . . . When I reached the county cricket ground the crowd was enormous. I paid my sixpence and in panic I rushed through the gates and round the ring of the congested spectators, as I heard the roaring at some flashing play I couldn't see. At last I crawled through a hole in the multitude and obtained a place on the grass. Tyldesley was still not out . . .

Although the professional was the backbone of county cricket, the amateur held his own. Moreover, famous amateur players still found it possible to combine the summer game with the tradition of public service; Alfred Lyttleton, who was Colonial Secretary in Balfour's administration, had been so fine a batsman that no less a critic than W. G. Grace described his stroke-play as 'the champagne of cricket'. The Hon. F. S.

Jackson, who captained England victoriously in the 1905 Test Matches against Australia, entered Parliament and ended his career as Governor of Bengal. An equally remarkable career was that of C. Aubrey Smith, who had played cricket for Sussex before becoming a matinée idol at the St James's Theatre and later emigrating to Hollywood.

Sport in which professionalism predominated drew the gate-money, but the amateur sportsmen retained public interest. Sir Laurence Jones, one-time President of the Oxford University Boat Club, writes:

In 1905 the Boat Race was still a National Institution. Every cab and bus driver in London tied a dark—or light—blue bow to his whip, every child wore a favour, and Frank Reynolds' ragged infant in a slum, back to the wall and half-throttled by the local Flashman, could still gasp out: 'No—not if you was to kill me I wouldn't be Cime-bridge.'

At Wimbledon the clothes and style of tennis were very different from today, but already coming events were casting a shadow, with Norman Brookes of Australia winning the Men's Singles and May Sutton of the USA carrying off the Women's.

Britain still dominated the Olympics, and the Olympics, then as now, were vexed by the metaphysical question: What is an amateur? The President of the British Olympic Association was Lord Desborough, a versatile sportsman, who had played cricket and run the mile for Harrow, rowed for Oxford in the famous tied boat race of 1877, and also distinguished himself as swordsman and mountaineer. The 1908 Games were opened

The first Test Match, 1909. Maclaren and Hobbs going out to bat

The Boat Race, 1909

at the White City on 13 July by Edward VII, who stood under an emblem, bearing the words 'Rex et Imperator', whilst 1,001 athletes filed past. Britain with 226 far exceeded the other competing countries; Denmark (126) came second in numbers, but her team included girl gymnasts, for whose displays no medals or points were awarded.

All the participating countries were European, apart from the Colonial teams from Australia, Canada and South Africa. C. B. Fry struck a discordant note by suggesting that, in future, the Games should be all-Imperial, except for the USA, which qualified, presumably, as an ex-Colonial. When the points were added up, the USA with 22 finished second to Britain with 38; but the sporting public had long taken this result for granted and its sentiments were monopolized by the plight of the Italian marathon walker, Durando Pietri, whom it persisted in calling Dorando. He had collapsed near the finish when in the lead and had been disqualified because in his semi-conscious state he had been helped to complete the course. Queen Alexandra rewarded his efforts by presenting a special gold cup to him and he received many offers to appear on the music hall stage.

Novelists, drawing on Edwardian childhoods, seem consistently to tell of long, hot summers and this has contributed to the legend of the Golden Age. One shares the illusion, as one studies the yellowing photographs of country-house parties, or the exemplary postures of the heroes of the cricket field. There he stands, L. C. H. Palairet, or A. C. Maclaren, his bat held high at the finish of a classic off-drive; transfixed for ever at the bowling crease, G. H. Hirst is poised to deliver the fast, swinging ball that will confound his Lancastrian foes. The shadow of the pavilion lengthens inch by inch across the ground and, as if in slow motion, the umpires stoop to remove the bails. The long, happy day is over and, in the words of the popular song of the Halls,

All go the same way home,
So there's no need to part at all.
We all go the same way home. . . .

But it is a longer way than many of them think and it goes by Ypres and Passchendaele.

Further Reading

Pound and Harmsworth, *Northcliffe*
A. M. Gollin, *The Observer and J. L. Garvin*
J. C. Trewin, *The Theatre Since 1900*
R. Findlater, *Banned*
C. MacInnes, *Sweet Saturday Night*
J. B. Booth, *Old Pink 'Un Days*
R. Low, *History of British Film*
N. Cardus, *Autobiography*

Short Bibliography

E. Nowell Smith (ed.), *Edwardian England*
Sir C. Petrie, *Scenes of Edwardian Life*
J. Bowle, *England: A Portrait*
Sir J. Clapham, *Economic History of Modern Britain*
R. S. Sayers, *A History of Economic Change*
Cole and Postgate, *The Common People*
A. Briggs (ed.), *They Saw It Happen*
I. Clephane, *Ourselves (1900–1930)*
J. Laver, *Taste and Fashion from the French Revolution until Today*
Sir L. Jones, *An Edwardian Youth*
S. Keppel, *Edwardian Daughter*
C. Chaplin, *My Autobiography*
H. G. Wells, *An Experiment in Autobiography*
Mackerness (ed.), *Journals of George Sturt*
V. Sackville-West, *The Edwardians*

Index

203